THE PREACHER AND SERMON PREPARATION

REVISED

The Preacher and Sermon Preparation

Revised Edition

Ian Fleck

AFRICA CHRISTIAN TEXTBOOKS

2017

The Preacher and Sermon Preparation
Revised Edition
© 1984, 2011, 2017 Ian Fleck

Africa Christian Textbooks (ACTS)

ACTS Bookshop, International HQ, TCNN,
PMB 2020, Bukuru, Plateau State, 930008, Nigeria
GSM: +234 (0) 803-589-5328; E-mail: info@acts-ng.com
Website: http://www.acts-ng.com

ISBN: 978-978-905-097-0 Print
ISBN: 978-978-905-320-9 ePub
ISBN: 978-978-905-321-6 Mobi

Scripture quotations are from the *Holy Bible, English Standard Version*, copyright © 2001 by Crossway Bibles, a publishing ministry of Good News Publishers. Used by permission. All rights reserved.

Revised edition 2011, 2017 © Africa Christian Textbooks
First edition *The Preacher and His Sermon* by Ian Fleck, 1984.
First published by Samuel Bill Theological College, Abak, Akwa Ibom State, Nigeria

CONTENTS

PREFACE TO THIRD EDITION

A third edition of this book has become necessary to facilitate a few necessary changes. No one is more surprised that I am that it has been in constant use for over thirty years.

Since the first publication of this book, the Revised Standard Version (RSV) on which the book was based has been revised in two editions; the New Revised Standard Version (NRSV) and the English Standard Version (ESV). The ESV has been chosen for all Scripture references.

The Apostle Paul said, "It pleased God through the folly of what we preach to save those who believe" 1 Corinthians 1:21. Therefore preachers are required for every generation, and this book is made available as a possible guide and starting-point for those at the beginning of their ministry, or to stimulate experienced preachers who may benefit from it.

Whilst its form and style continues to change, preaching remains a vital part of the life of most congregations. Writers on the subject of preaching are unanimous in regard to the value of expository preaching. All agree that it is the most effective way of proclaiming the Word of God and there are benefits for the preacher and the congregation. It awakens an interest in the study of the Scriptures and helps to solve many of the problems of life. The expository method of Bible study seeks to present truths, concepts and principles that are taught by a Scripture passage.

This small book is a guide designed for those who have sensed God's call upon their lives to preach His Word. My prayer is that it will continue to be used by the next generation of preachers.

Ian Fleck, Ballymena, N. Ireland, February 2017

INTRODUCTION

If you have never prepared or preached a sermon, this book gives you in simple terms how to begin. If you are an experienced preacher, it may stimulate and refresh your idea of preaching, or awaken you to some deficiencies in your work.

Preaching is only for those who have been called to the work and have been sent forth with the gift of preaching. Reading and studying these notes will not make anyone a successful preacher unless he has been commissioned by the Lord. Only God can give someone the gift of preaching. But as you "earnestly desire the higher gifts" (1 Cor 12:31), it is the prayer of the author and the publishers that this book will be used by God to help readers to know their calling and to develop this gift that is so important for the spread of the gospel and the building up of the church.

Many students find Homiletics a very difficult subject. They complain that it is too hard for them to prepare sermons, and are surprised that so much is involved. The accusation has been made that a preacher does little work (and sometimes it is implied also that he does not deserve a high salary). However, where the preacher is serious and conscientious he will be a very busy man. He will spend much time every day in his study in prayer and preparation for preaching (cf. Mark 1:35-39; Acts 6:4).

There are many opinions among experienced preachers how sermons should be prepared. This book does not claim to cover all methods. It grew out of the author's nine years ministry in Nigeria, lecturing and discussing in the classroom, and listening to hundreds of messages in college chapel services as well as church services and conferences. If you have your own method and are convinced it is good, then continue. But if you have no method and do not know how to begin, then try the methods outlined in these notes and make every effort to do it to the very best of your ability.

The college graduate or experienced preacher will not find much that is new, as originality for the methods or statements is not claimed. The reason that they are in this form is because of the lack of suitable books in the market. Numerous headings and divisions are used throughout to make it easier for both student and teacher to study this great subject in sections as time permits. It also helps the student to understand the subject more easily and remember what he is studying.

It is a solemn thing to preach the gospel. This work cannot be undertaken by anyone who is not prepared to suffer and labour. It is a high calling and it involves much preparation and many sacrifices. May the God who commands us to "go and make disciples of all nations" use this book to help those who desire to be more effective in the great commission of proclaiming the Word of God to needy people.

Ian Fleck, SBTC, Abak, 1984.

THE DEFINITION OF CHRISTIAN PREACHING

Since the days of Moses, Samuel, Elijah and the prophets, we have had men who have preached to the human race. Often these men proclaimed divine truths and messages from the holy and just God to His chosen people. At times, they declared God's judgment and punishment on a rebellious and wicked people, and at other times, they gave messages of encouragement and blessing.

In the New Testament, preaching is the proclaiming of the good news of salvation. In Acts 5:42 we read about the early Christians, "Every day in the temple and from house to house, they did not cease teaching and preaching Jesus as the Christ." Paul said, "We preach Christ crucified" (1 Corinthians 1:23). Again, he said, "If I preach the gospel, that gives me no ground for boasting. For necessity is laid upon me. Woe to me if I do not preach the gospel" (1 Corinthians 9:16).

A man can stand before an audience and speak about politics, economics, health or farming, and his hearers listen carefully to his message but that is not preaching. The great need in our churches today is for true Biblical preaching.

A famous preacher said, "To me the work of preaching is the highest and the greatest and the most glorious calling to which anyone can ever be called." We need preachers who will "preach Christ crucified." We need preachers who will "preach Jesus as the Christ." Failure to do this, is failure as a preacher, and is not preaching at all.

Where there is true preaching people will come and listen to it. There is something deep in the heart and soul of man that wants to hear what the preacher is saying. If people are not attending our Churches, then we should not look for the fault among the people, but the preachers. Do the preachers have a relevant and meaningful message for the people? If so, the people will come to hear it.

Preaching should make such a difference to the hearer that his whole life is changed. Preaching should help those who are troubled, depressed or anxious about anything. True Biblical preaching will save the pastor much time in his pastoral work. Many preachers spend much of their time dealing with individual and family problems among their people. This could be greatly reduced, if their preaching from the pulpit was what it should be.

The faithful preaching of the Word of God, applied by the power of the Holy Spirit, will give the individual who is listening, the answer to many of his problems. He gets the advice and help that the person needs which could only come from a personal pastoral visit. So without seeking his pastor the person in need has found help through the Word of God by faithful preaching.

Preaching is God's appointed way of spreading the gospel message and it cannot be replaced by anything. When people come to Church, they have not come for entertainment with the preacher being the entertainer. When the standard of preaching falls, the standard of the Church falls, and the standard of the life of the individual Christian falls.

Let us, therefore, raise the standard of preaching in our Churches. Let it have a central place in the life and work of the Church, as it has been in the New Testament Church. May we hold preaching with the highest regard as Jesus did, and prepare our sermons in the belief that they can change the lives of many people for eternity.

The Need for Preachers

"And he (Jesus) appointed twelve (whom he also named apostles) so that they might be with him and he might send them out to preach" (Mark 3:14). It is God's plan that the gospel is known through preaching. Therefore, there will always be the need for preachers to preach the gospel. In Romans 10:14-15 we read, "How then will they call on him in whom they have not believed? And how are they to believe in him of whom they have never heard? And how are they to hear without someone preaching? And how are they to preach unless they are sent?" As long as the world exists, there will be the need for preachers. Only those who have been "sent" by God should go. Not every Christian has been called by God to be a preacher. If a man decides that he wants to be a preacher because he likes to talk to people or the honour of such a job, he is sure to fall, for such a person goes in human strength, not in the power that God gives His servants.

The need for preachers is great all over the world. This is why Jesus said, "The harvest is plentiful, but the labourers are few; therefore pray earnestly to the Lord of the harvest to send out labourers into his harvest" (Matthew 9:37-38). When we consider that millions of people in the world today have never heard the name of Jesus Christ, and know nothing of His redeeming love, we need to pray more, and seek to do all that we can do to preach to them the gospel message.

Assignment:

1. What is preaching and why can it not be replaced by anything?
2. What is the difference between preaching a sermon and giving a public speech or address?
3. Why is it true that every Christian should be a witness for Christ, but not every Christian should be a preacher?
4. Why do people want to listen to a preacher?
5. What would you say is the greatest need in our churches today?

THE QUALIFICATIONS OF A PREACHER

A doctor studies medicine and a carpenter learns to work with wood. For someone to undertake a job or profession he needs to be qualified in some way to do it. What then are the qualifications of a preacher? As the work of the preacher is the most important work in the world then he must be qualified for that work. As we cannot separate a preacher from his preaching, we need to look at a few of his essential qualifications. Every preacher should examine his life and qualifications for the work.

1. The preacher must be a Christian

It is very important that the preacher is a Christian. But it has been known for someone to be a preacher and not be a Christian. For them preaching is a job, it is their means of livelihood. They have studied at a Bible College with the same attitude as someone would study medicine or law at a College.

How can someone lead a soul to Christ if he has not travelled that way himself? Jesus said to Nicodemus, a religious and moral person, that "unless one is born again he cannot see the kingdom of God" (John 3:3). Only the person who has experienced the new birth for himself can speak from experience and authority to the unbelievers. Otherwise, it is "the blind leading the blind."

The person who can humbly and honestly say, "But I am not ashamed, for I know whom I have believed, and I am convinced that he is able to guard until that Day what has been entrusted to me," (2 Tim. 1:12) will be the person who can assure his hearers that he knows what he is talking about. He will impress them of his own confidence in the salvation he preaches.

2. The preacher must have a love for Christ

Jesus said to Simon Peter, "Simon, son of John, do you love me more than these?" He said to Him, "Yes, Lord; you know that I love you," He said to him, "Feed my lambs" (John 21:15). Here our Lord showed how necessary it is to love Him before we can feed His lambs.

No one can be a servant of Jesus Christ and feed His sheep if that person does not have a love for his Master. The more the preacher loves Christ the more he will want to preach to others about the love Christ had for us, "In that while we were still sinners, Christ died for us" (Romans 5:8).

As the preacher sees the love of Christ, he is encouraged and forced to tell others about Him. The preacher who is living close to his Saviour will love Him, and this love will be seen by others, and cause them to want to know more about Christ.

3. The preacher must be a man of prayer

When we look at the life of Christ, we see that He lived a life of prayer. He prayed early in the morning, He prayed through the night; He prayed for His enemies; He prayed for His disciples; He prayed for those in trouble, and He prayed when He was in Gethsemane before His crucifixion.

Therefore, the preacher must be a man of prayer. The preacher who does not have the interest, or take the time to pray for the families and individuals to whom he will preach, cannot exhort them to follow the ways of God with all his heart. He must pray for them before he can preach to them, and appeal to them to take heed to the Word of God.

The preacher who prepares his sermons through his own wisdom and knowledge will fail, but the man who seeks God, will have a message from the Lord to his people. God cannot use a prayerless sermon, nor can the preacher be guided by the Holy Spirit, as he would be when he prays over his message.

The preacher must also pray that his own life be an example for others to follow. It is not good for a preacher to say one thing and do another. His life should support and reinforce what he preaches. He needs to pray for courage and strength to carry out his duties, for guidance in his work and "pray constantly, giving thanks in all circumstances; for this is the will of God in Christ Jesus…"

4. The preacher must study the Bible

The man who is going to preach from the Bible should be a man who studies it. He must study, not only just to get a message for his congregation; but for his own spiritual growth. The Word of God must be the meat and drink to his own soul.

When taking our daily food it is not just a drink of milk or a cake. If we want to be strong physically then we need to eat other food, and some meat takes a lot of chewing. It is the same with our spiritual life; we need to feed on God's Word and sometimes it takes hard work studying and thinking about it. Again if we want to be strong physically we eat more than once a week, but sad to say some Christians only feed their spiritual life once a week, with the sermon in the Church.

The preacher should have a general knowledge of what the whole Bible contains. He should have an idea of the contents of every book from Genesis to Revelation, and should commit to memory important verses and passages. This will help him as he preaches, counsels and talks to people about spiritual things. Some people may say that this is hard work, which is true, but then we are dealing with very important matters and a very special Book. Knowledge of the Bible does not come by occasional reading of a few verses. It is a result of much patient work from an earnest and obedient heart.

To understand the Bible, and for the Holy Spirit to teach us new truths, we need to be obedient to what He says to us. If the Holy Spirit through the Bible teaches us to do something and we do not obey, then the Holy Spirit will not keep revealing new truths to us until we are obedient.

5. The preacher must be blameless in his life

Paul wrote to Titus and said,

> For an overseer, as God's steward, must be above reproach. He must not be arrogant or quick-tempered or a drunkard or violent or greedy for gain, but hospitable, a lover of good, self-controlled, upright, holy, and disciplined. He must hold firm to the trustworthy word as taught, so that he may be able to give instruction in sound doctrine and also to rebuke those who contradict (Titus 1:7-9).

Many people watch the life of the preacher as well as listen to his sermons. In fact, his life is not a private matter. Damage can be brought to the cause of Christ through failure in a preacher's life, more than anything else. When a preacher's life falls below the standard that is required of him then the unbeliever has much to rejoice about, and uses this as an excuse to remain in his sins or he turns further against Christianity and wants nothing to do with it.

The Bible says, "You know that we who teach shall be judged with greater strictness" (James 3:1). Therefore, we have a greater responsibility to live lives that are blameless and above reproach.

6. The preacher must be called by God

In Romans 10:14-15 we read, "How are they to hear without someone preaching? And how are they to preach unless they are sent?" Again in 1 Corinthians 12:4-5 we read, "Now there are varieties of gifts, but the same Spirit; and there are varieties of service, but the same Lord." Therefore a preacher should be a person who has received that gift, and been sent by God.

It is wrong for someone to take up the work of a preacher because a Church suggests it to him or because he would like to do the job. He needs to seek the Lord and search his heart to make sure he has the gift of preaching, and the call from God. Not all Christians are meant to be preachers. A preacher is not a Christian who decided to preach, but should be a man who can do nothing else because of the conviction within his heart. If a man is happy doing another work then God has not called him to be a preacher. If a man finds satisfaction doing anything else other than preaching and can stay away from it, then he should. But if he has no peace of mind, and is not able to hold back the desire or resist it, then he should follow that conviction within his heart.

The work of a preacher is not easy, so when he faces times of difficulty then he looks back to his calling and knows that he did not take this work upon himself but that God called him, and will support him in his time of need.

7. The preacher must be able for the work

Sometimes a young man may come to his Church leaders and say, "I believe God has called me to be a preacher." What does the Church look for in a man who says he is called to be a preacher?

a. **He should be "filled with the Spirit."** That is the first and greatest requirement. When the early Church in Acts 6 needed workers they were to "choose seven men from among you who are known to be full of the Spirit and Wisdom." The person must have proved himself to be a sincere Christian. And as Paul wrote, "He must not be a recent convert, or he may become puffed up with conceit." (1 Timothy 3:6).

b. **He should be able to teach.** A person, who cannot talk properly or clearly for people to understand, cannot preach to a gathering of people. A person who cannot express his thoughts clearly, will not be able to present his sermon in such a way that the hearer can follow. Therefore, if a person comes to the Church and says that God has called him to be a preacher, when the Church knows that he is not capable of teaching or expressing himself clearly, they have a duty to point out to him that he should consider again God's will for his life and perhaps think about other work.

c. **He should be capable of dealing with difficulties.** If a man is always struggling with difficulties and problems in his own life then he is not capable of helping others. If he always has spiritual problems himself, then he cannot counsel others who have spiritual problems. If he is not in control of his own family and life then he cannot set an example for others. "How can the blind lead the blind" is the question we must ask? Therefore, the preacher must be a man who is mature and has experience in life.

d. **He should have some training.** We have already seen that the preacher should be a Christian and a person who studies his Bible. But if someone is going to preach the Word of God to a congregation where you have educated and learned people, he needs some special training. He should know how to handle concordances and Bible dictionaries so that he is accurate in what he is saying. As well as a general knowledge of the Scripture, he needs to study it in a systematic manner, and study Bible Theology.

It is also very profitable to study the history of the Church. Examine heresies that have come into the Church and their danger. Examine revivals and be encouraged by their results and blessings. We can learn much from the failings and successes of the Church down through the years.

8. The preacher must have a concern for others

A man may be well qualified in many ways to be a preacher. He may have studied theology for three or more years in a Bible College, but if he does not have a love for the sinner then he will be a failure. A person may be a great preacher and love preaching but he needs to have an interest in people; he needs to have a concern for others and their spiritual condition.

Jesus showed us His compassion and concern for others. When His disciples wanted Him to eat, He said, "My food is to do the will of him who sent me and to accomplish his work," (John 4:32-38). This was because many people were coming out of the city of Samaria and He had a concern for them. He did not feel physically hungry having a strong desire to help them spiritually.

Paul reminds us that we may have many gifts, but unless we have love, we are nothing (1 Corinthians 13). The preacher must have a love for the souls of men and women and have the words of Jesus burning in his breast, "For what does it profit a man to gain the whole world and forfeit his soul?" (Mark 8:36). The preacher needs to see the value of a soul and the work he is called to do.

Assignment:

1. Why is it necessary for a preacher to be a Christian?
2. What did Jesus ask Peter before He told him to feed His lambs?
3. A preacher can preach a good sermon even though he doesn't pray over it. Discuss.
4. Can a man be a good preacher and pastor without studying the Bible?
5. Surely a preacher's life is a personal affair and he can be successful irrespective of how he lives. Discuss.
6. Can a man just decide he wants to become a preacher and start the work?
7. What special qualifications are needed for a preacher?

LESSON 3

THE TEXT

The portion of Scripture chosen from which a sermon is developed is called the text. This text may consist of several verses, one verse or part of a verse of Scripture. Some preachers prepare their sermons and then look for a text and Bible reading to go with it. This is a very wrong way to do it.

The sermon should be an exposition of the Word of God. Therefore, the first thing the preacher needs to do is to select the portion of Scripture he wants to expound to his hearers.

1. A text keeps the message Biblical

When the preacher starts with a text then his message is going to be centred on the Word of God. This is very important, as the hearer has come to hear a message from the Lord. The preacher however, must be careful that he does not go away from the text and use it only as a starting point. He must develop the message from the text and use it throughout as his reference point.

2. A text gives the message authority

That which gives a message authority is the Word of God. A preacher who just gets up and talks for thirty minutes without referring to the

Scriptures does not know that "For the word of God is living and active, sharper than any two-edged sword, piercing to the division of soul and of spirit, of joints and of marrow, and discerning the thoughts and intentions of the heart" (Hebrews 4:12).

3. A text gives variety in sermons

When a preacher selects a text and prepares a message from it, then it will be different from the last message he prepared from another text. This makes the preacher prepare a variety of messages week after week. It also means the congregation is getting a variety of messages and as a result is taught more of the Scriptures. There are preachers, however, who seem to be able to preach the same sermon no matter what text has been chosen. But if this is the case then the preacher is not preparing his sermon from the text and needs to study carefully the next section entitled "Understanding the text."

4. The Selection of the Text

This selection of a text is a very important matter. A number of things should be considered when choosing the text for a sermon.

4.1. Consider the congregation

The preacher should consider the congregation where he is going to preach. Is it the Sunday morning service? Is it the mid-week Bible Study or Christian class? Is it a convention? Is it a youth meeting; a men's meeting or a women's meeting? Is the meeting in a township church or in a bush church?

The preacher should consider these things so that the message he brings to the people will be a message they will understand and be helpful to them. The wise preacher will prepare his sermon with his congregation in mind. If he is asked to be the visiting speaker at a meeting, he should know exactly what kind of meeting it is, so that he can prepare his message accordingly.

4.2. The text should have a clear meaning

Sometimes preachers choose texts that are difficult to understand, or from which it is very hard to make a sermon. But, as often is the case, the sermon they preach does not develop from that text. They select the text but the sermon is not connected to it and could easily be preached from any other part of the Bible.

The Bible is full of texts, and there are enough with a clear meaning and message to keep any preaching going for a lifetime. Why then select difficult and obscure passages? The preacher must be careful; however, that he does not neglect any part of the Bible or doctrine. He is responsible to preach all the truth that is contained in the Scriptures.

4.3. Choose texts that have a complete thought

Although the text may be a verse, part of a verse or a number of verses, it should express a complete thought. One of the reasons why false cults can get proof for their beliefs is because they take phrases out of the Bible that do not express a complete thought. They then use this to say what they believe and want to say.

The preacher must be careful when choosing his texts so that they give clear thought and positive teaching of the Word of God. The sermon explains in detail that meaning and teaching, to the spiritual growth of the hearer.

4.4. Consider the exposition of a book

The preacher should take a book of the Bible and expound it section by section. Sometimes the sections may be only a verse and other times a paragraph or several verses.

This gives consistent teaching to the congregation, which will help them greatly understand the Word of God. It means that the preacher knows exactly where his text must come from. He can also teach many things that could be difficult for him to teach, if he was just taking texts at various places in the Bible.

4.5. Keep a notebook for texts

The preacher who is serious about his work will keep a notebook beside him when reading the Bible. Whenever a verse, thought or illustration comes to him, he should write it down.

Frequently the preacher can turn to this book, think about these verses and as the thoughts come to mind then write them down below that text. Then one day when the Holy Spirit guides him, he can use one of these texts from his notebook, with all the comments and thoughts attached to it, and prepare the sermon.

The preacher, who keeps adding new verses to his notebook and his own thoughts with them, will have a good supply of material for sermons. It also means that if he is suddenly called upon to preach somewhere he can quickly prepare a message for that occasion.

Assignment:

1.   Why is it good for a preacher to use a text for his sermon?
2.   What should a preacher consider when selecting a text to preach at a meeting?
3.   What are the requirements of a good text?
4.   What are the advantages of the exposition of a chapter or book of the Bible?
5.   How should a preacher read his Bible?

UNDERSTANDING THE TEXT

Now that the preacher has decided on the text, he needs to prepare his sermon. This is usually a difficult task. Many young preachers give up in despair because they just cannot get a sermon outline from their text, and prepare a sermon from another text that is easier.

If, however, we watch a carpenter at his work he will not give up if the two pieces of wood do not make a good joint at his first attempt. Rather, with his plane, or chisel or saw he will remove a small piece of wood here and small piece there, until the two pieces fit together and make a perfect joint.

The preacher, who gives up with his first attempt of knowing what the text says, or of making the outline of a sermon from the text, does not understand the labour that is involved in preparing a sermon. A preacher who does not spend time in the careful preparation of his sermon will say only a few comments about the text, which will do very little for the spiritual growth of the hearer.

It is the responsibility of the preacher to work at the text until he understands what it is saying. He needs to ask the question "What is this text saying?" "What does it mean?" "How can I explain its meaning to others?" The answers to these questions are not easy to get, but he must have the answers before preaching the sermon.

There is no easy way to prepare a sermon. We cannot follow a few simple rules and as a result have a sermon ready for preaching in 15 or 30 minutes. Therefore, for anyone to suggest certain rules can be both dangerous and misleading. However, we can learn something from the experiences of others, and if we put these suggestions into practice, it will be a great help to the young preacher.

1. Read the passage

After the preacher has waited on the Lord for his text, he needs to prayerfully read the passage many times. Reading only the text is not enough. He needs to make sure he is reading enough before and after the text to give the full meaning of it. To read the whole chapter may not be enough. Sometimes the thought or context of the passage starts in the chapter before or sometimes it continues into the chapter after, the one in which our text is found.

It is good to read the passage in different versions of the Bible, as new thoughts may come to us from the different translations. Therefore, before the preacher is ready to prepare his sermon he should read the passage several times, and if possible, in different versions of the Bible.

2. Understand the words correctly

God has revealed Himself and His message through words. It is therefore important to know the exact meaning of the words used. Look carefully at the tense of the words used. Are they past, present or future tense? Are they singular or plural? Where have the words been used before and what did they mean there? Do they mean the same here?

To do this very well we should understand Hebrew and Greek, but where this knowledge is lacking, the preacher can find help from a number of sources. A Hebrew – English or Greek – English interlinear Old or New Testament can prove most useful, where a literal translation of the original writings is given. An Expository Dictionary of Old Testament or New Testament words will help explain the meaning of words used. A Young's Analytical Concordance of the Bible will help the preacher find other references in the Bible where the same word is used. It will show the different Hebrew or Greek words used for the one word in English … at times it is very useful and important to notice this difference.

A good example of this is seen in the conversation between Jesus and Peter in John 21:15-17. Different Greek words are used, but both translated to mean "Love" in English. In Greek, one word means "deep sacrificial love" and the other means "brotherly love or affection." When Jesus asked Peter if he loved Him, Jesus used the first word but Peter answered with the second. But the third time Jesus used the second word, and this grieved Peter because Jesus had now lowered the standard or quality of the word "love." This difference is not seen in the English word "love" and the wrong meaning can be taken from the text.

It is therefore very important to check the meaning of the words in the original even though we understand the meaning of the English words. Sometimes, the English language is not able to show the different meaning. In addition, over the years, some of the English words in the King James Version of the Bible have changed their meaning so that they do not mean the same today as they meant when that translation was made. Therefore, we need to know the real meaning of the passage and the best words we can use today to express it.

3. Understand the place or events that are happening

It is important to know something about the places described in our text. If we know that Athens where Paul visited was a centre of learning, and the monuments showed that in the past it had been a very prosperous city, it will help us understand Paul's situation.

Again, it is useful to know that Corinth was a very prosperous city in the 8th Century B.C., when it was the centre of industry, trade and commerce. But it was completely destroyed in 146 B.C. Later, in Roman times, it was a city of wealth and freedom to do as one desired. To live as a Corinthian meant to live in luxury and immorality. As it was an important seaport it was a meeting place of all nationalities, and it offered for everyone all kinds of pleasure.

With this kind of background knowledge one can understand more fully, the former lives of those who became Christian, and the problems the church had in Corinth.

Again, if we can follow Abraham's journey from Ur of the Chaldeas to Canaan and Egypt, or know about the enemy nations that surrounded the Israelites it will help us to understand much more fully the stories in the Bible concerning these events.

Much of the information we require can be obtained from a Bible Handbook. It is a guide to the Bible, and gives useful background information that is helpful to fully understand the place, or events taking place, in the portion of Scripture we are studying.

4. Understand what the passage meant when it was written and to whom it was spoken

It is important to interpret a verse or passage in the light of the circumstances in which it originally took place. Read the complete passage carefully and study other portions or Scriptures that deal with the same period or events. Many of the events during the time of the prophets are better understood when we know what is happening from the Historical books of Kings, Chronicles, Ezra and Nehemiah.

In this way, we can understand the life and circumstances of the events concerning our passage, and we can think more clearly of what the writer or speaker was trying to say. Also, what the readers or hearers understand him to be saying.

We cannot understand the message of any of the prophets unless we know the circumstances in which they worked. The prophets made their messages relevant to their audiences. So we today need to know the situation and condition and make our own preaching relevant to the needs of the people to whom we preach.

Much damage can be done when the preacher does not understand what the writer meant, because he did not take the time to read and study, and try to understand the original meaning. It is good to know the purpose of the book, that is, why the author wrote the book, or the Epistle, and examine the text in the light of this knowledge.

5. Understand the text in the light of its context

The context is what comes before and what follows our text. To find the real context the preacher may have to read the chapter before or the chapter after the text, to know clearly what the writer is saying. The text or passage of Scripture can only be fully understood in the light of the complete book from which it is taken. Therefore, the whole book should be read in several translations, so that we know exactly why the book was written, and therefore what this passage we are considering means.

When the writer says "Therefore" or "Then," he is joining two thoughts together. "As a result of what I have said 'therefore' I now say this" or "Because this has happened 'Then' this is the result." So there is no way we can fully understand what the author is saying unless we read and study the complete section dealing with this matter, which may take several chapters or the whole book.

One of the reasons why we have so many sects and false teaching in the world today is because someone has taken a verse from the Bible out of its context and put his own interpretation on it. As a result, we are taught one side of a doctrine, which is only a half-truth and not the complete truth. It is dangerous and wrong to preach from a verse without taking into consideration the circumstances and statements surrounding it.

Let us look at John 9:3 to show the importance of knowing the context. The verse reads "It was not that this man sinned, or his parents, …" (E.S.V.). In the A.V. it reads "neither hath this man sinned nor his parents." Does this mean that we have three people here who have never sinned - this man and his parents? However, in Romans 3:23 we read, "All have sinned and fall short of the glory of God." So how do we explain this difference? We see it in the context of our verses. In John 9:2 it says "Rabbi, who sinned, this man or his parents THAT HE WAS BORN BLIND?" To this question, Jesus gives the answer "It (that is the blindness) was not the result of any sin committed by this man or his parents…"

In Romans 5:1 Paul says, "Therefore since we have been justified by faith, we have peace with God…" Here the "therefore" refers to what the apostle was writing about concerning faith in chapter 4. By taking a text out of its context, we can get the Bible to contradict itself and say something that is wrong and not Biblical. The context makes clear what the author is saying in the passage we have chosen as our text.

6. Understand the text in the light of the whole Bible

No text stands on its own as it is part of a chapter, which is part of a book that is part of the Bible. The more one studies the Bible the more it is seen to be a complete unit and not a collection of isolated texts and messages.

It is very important to develop a general knowledge of the whole Bible. The whole Bible should be read frequently, at least once a year, to keep the mind fresh with the overall teaching of Scripture.

Someone can read, "you see that a person is justified by works" (James 2:24) and start to teach that we can be saved by our works. Unless he understands the circumstances in which James wrote this; examines the context of the verse, and can remember that Paul wrote "By grace you are saved through faith," he is going to teach a false doctrine.

Again, when we read Acts 20:36, we see that Paul "knelt down and prayed." We may teach that we must pray on our knees, unless we remember that Nehemiah stood and prayed before King Artaxerxes, and Hezekiah prayed while lying on his sick bed.

We should be prepared to look to the Old Testament to help understand the New Testament, or study the fuller revelation in the New Testament to explain some passages in the Old Testament. No doctrine or truth is taught from only one verse of the Bible. If we are prepared to search the Scriptures, we will find those other verses and passages that will help to explain, and expand the truth mentioned in our text. The man who turns first to a commentary to find the meaning of his text has made a mistake. His first step should be to search the Scriptures to throw more light on the passage he is considering.

Assignment:

1. Does a preacher need to read and study more than the text when preparing a sermon?
2. Why is it necessary to examine the words in the text?
3. If someone says he can prepare a good sermon without knowing the background to the text, would you agree with him?
4. Is it necessary to understand the text in the light of its context?
5. A sermon can be prepared from a text without having a general knowledge of the Bible. Discuss.

LESSON 5

THE THEME

Before a preacher can prepare a sermon, he needs to know the theme he is going to consider from the text he has chosen. More than one theme may be taken from a text but we cannot have more than one theme in a sermon. For example, look at John 3:16 "For God so loved the world that He gave His only Son, that whoever believes in Him should not perish but have eternal life." Several sermons could be preached on the following themes:

a.   "The Great **Love** of God"
b.   "God **gave** His only Son"
c.   "He who **believes** shall not perish"
d.   "Eternal life is available for **all**"

Each sermon would be different as the theme is different and the emphasis is placed on a different truth found in the text. We could say that the sermon is the theme expanded to what we say in 30 minutes, and the theme is the sermon reduced into a single statement.

The theme from the text must be exactly what the preacher is going to use to preach his sermon. On the other hand, his finished sermon should be exactly what he had taken as his theme from the text. Many preachers tell us their theme at the beginning of the sermon, but as they preach we have no idea as to what they are talking about. In reality, their sermon was never developed with the theme in mind but is something entirely different.

The theme is the thought or idea that is running through the sermon from start to finish. So if we take a) "The Great Love of God" as our theme, then we preach on the "love" of God and that thought runs through the sermon. On the other hand, if we take c) "He who believes shall not perish" as our theme, then the need to "believe" and the results will be the thought that is considered in the sermon.

The theme guides the preacher and keeps his mind thinking in one direction. If someone preaches from John 3:16 without his thoughts on a theme to guide him, then it is almost certain all of the above four themes will be contained in that one sermon. It will make it difficult for the preacher to know exactly where he is putting his emphasis; and the hearer will find it difficult to know what the preacher is trying to say as he is saying so much, and is not limiting himself to one theme found in the text.

Careful consideration must be given to the selection and wording of the theme. It is only after several readings of the text and its context, and thoughtful study as to what aspect of the text we are going to consider, can the theme be chosen. When the theme is chosen then prepare the sermon with that thought in mind, and do not be side tracked to something else.

There is a difference between a "theme" and a "subject." A subject covers much more than a theme. We can speak of the general subject "Science," but that can be separated into different sections or "thoughts" of science, e.g. Chemical, Physical, Political, Agricultural and Natural.

In a theological college or seminary students study the subject "Doctrine" but this is divided into different parts of "thoughts" e.g.

Doctrine of God, Doctrine of Christ, Doctrine of Man, Doctrine of Salvation, and the Doctrine of the Church.

When preparing a sermon on a subject we search the Bible to get all the references dealing with the subject. But the "theme" of a textual sermon is the "thought" we are dealing with, taken from that text.

Assignment:

1. What does the word "theme" mean?
2. Why is it good to have a theme for a sermon?
3. How does someone find the theme of a text?
4. If you were preaching a sermon on Romans 6:23, what would be your theme?
5. Write the theme for two sermons on 2 Corinthians 5:17.

LESSON 6

THE DISCUSSION OR BODY OF THE SERMON

We have decided on the theme which is the "thought" or "idea" that is in our text; now we are going to discuss, explain and expand that "thought" in our sermon. It is very important that this is done properly, or we will fail, as preachers to teach and instruct the things of God, to those who sit in our congregations.

We may know what we want to say but the questions we must ask ourselves are, How do I say it? How do I explain this? Who am I talking to? Are they old or young, believer or unbeliever, those in trouble or in need?

Therefore, we must present the sermon in a clear and simple way, so that everyone can understand what we are saying. The best way to do this is to prepare the sermon in such a way that we have a plan that gives an organized presentation of the material. If our thoughts are not put into order, then what we deliver will give confusion and make it very difficult for the hearer to understand.

1. Write down the thoughts

Having thought about the text, the context, the background, the circumstances in which it was written, the proper meaning of the words used, and the general teaching of the Bible, we start to put all this information either down on paper or into a computer. We write it down in any order. We write down this information and our thoughts and explanations in brief form. If we don't write them down as they come to our mind we will forget much useful information that could be used for the sermon, but when the time comes we have forgotten that idea. It could have been a good illustration and therefore a great loss to the sermon.

The preacher turns the central thought over and over in his mind. He asks questions – What? Where? When? Who? How? - to make his mind think. He jots down all these ideas and thoughts just as they come, without any consideration given to order or expression. Allow the mind to be free as it thinks out the good and not so good, the useful and the useless, the important and the unimportant.

When a man is going to build a house, he gathers together all his materials. The sand, cement, stones, blocks, wood, zinc, nails, windows and doors are all brought to the building site – some he will use at the beginning and others he will use at the end. He does not place them in any order, the sand, stones, and blocks are placed near the site and the other materials are locked into a shed to be kept safe. The preacher also gathers all his materials to build a sermon just as the builder gathers his materials before building a house.

2. Have an outline

The first thing the builder does is to look at his plan. He needs to know what he is to build with all this material lying around. Is he to build a house, or school or church? The plan will tell him the size and shape of the building, and when he has put all this material together, he has a building just like the picture of the one in the plan. Therefore, the preacher also needs a plan to use the material that he has gathered.

If the builder has no plan and starts to build with no thought of what the plan is, or in his mind of the finished work, he will build something that is like "nothing" and good for nothing. The same with the preacher, if he starts preaching and just uses up his material without a plan, the hearer will not know what he is doing and end up with a sermon that has not served any useful purpose.

Drawing the plans for a house is a slow job. All the rooms are to fit together; the doors are to be put in the right place or the room is useless, and the windows in the right place to let in the light. The architect constantly changes his plans until he is satisfied that everything fits together and is in its right place, thus making the building complete and satisfactory. The same principle applies to the building of a sermon. We work at the plan until we get it complete and satisfactory.

The preacher looks at the material he has gathered and starts putting it under different headings. A thought here and a thought there, which he had previously noted can now be brought together, as they are seen to deal with the same idea, or are similar in content. Now other thoughts are brought together into another group, as they deal with another idea and are similar in content. This is continued until all, or almost all of our thoughts and notes have been grouped together. Sometimes we will have something noted that we cannot put into a group. We leave these out and use them on another occasion when we are preparing another sermon with a different theme.

The headings or divisions may be numbered 1, 2, 3 etc. And the different thoughts under the headings may be numbered a), b), c) etc. It is important that the headings or divisions come naturally from the text. Each division should be clear and different from the other divisions and show progressive thought about the text with the theme in mind.

Some preachers think it is only a waste of time spending hours trying to get an outline for his sermon. It seems he is making no progress and wants to do something that makes him think he is doing well. Therefore, he starts to write out his sermon without "wasting the time" of preparing an outline. As a result, his thoughts are not in order and after a short time, he no longer has anything to write.

Other times he remembers something he should have said near the beginning but there is no way he can include it now in that place. He now convinces himself that he has his sermon prepared and leaves his study to do other things.

When Sunday comes he starts to preach this sermon he has "prepared," but after ten minutes he no longer has anything new to say about the text. He starts to repeat what he has said already or say things that are not connected to his text or the theme he had in mind. As a result, the congregation is not getting the best and often hearing the same remarks and statements week after week.

3. The Value of divisions

The divisions are the sections or groups in which we have gathered together our thoughts and notes. It is very important to have these divisions, if our sermon is to be properly thought out and made. Making the divisions is very difficult but the value of them is great.

3.1. The divisions help the preacher

When the preacher is preparing his sermon he is constantly thinking what this text is saying and how he can explain that to his congregation.

a.   The divisions help the preacher to gather his thoughts and information together, in an orderly way as he seeks to understand all the text is saying. If a sermon is going to explain a text in detail, then it should be prepared in such a way that nothing is neglected or left out. The divisions help the preacher to do this.

b. The divisions keep the preacher to his theme. If the preacher has his theme in his mind as he prepares his sermon, then each division is connected in some way to that theme. A sermon that is prepared with divisions, and each division is a step further in explaining the text, with the theme in mind, then the preacher cannot wander away into another thought or illustration that has no connection with his text.

c. The divisions help the preacher to preach his sermon. A sermon that is clearly outlined can help the preacher remember what he is going to say. His thoughts and words flow freely as he preaches, because he has the division in his mind and knows exactly how he is step by step going to explain his text. So the divisions help his memory and he knows what he wants to say next.

3.2. The divisions help the hearer

Great care must be taken when dividing up the sermon into divisions, because they help the hearer. Anything that is helpful to the hearer must be done to the best of our ability and time taken to make sure it is done well.

a. The divisions help the hearer take in the truth. The hearer listens to the sermon so that he can learn more about the Word of God. If the sermon has been divided up carefully, and each division is a new thought, then the hearer will find it easier to take in the truth about that text.

b.   The divisions help the hearer understand what the preacher is saying. If a preacher preaches for 20 minutes with no order or divisions in his sermon, it is very difficult for the hearer to understand what he is saying. If the sermon has divisions, then the hearer can understand much better what the preacher is trying to say about the text.

c.   The divisions help the hearer to remember what has been said. When the voice of the preacher is silent the divisions help the hearer remember what he has said. When the hearer leaves the Church, he will be able to remember at least one or two of the divisions in the preacher's sermon and it may be the answer to his need or problem when he goes home.

Note of warning: Although the divisions help the majority of people who are listening to the sermon to follow what is said, that may not always be the case. Elderly people may not be thinking in this way, and find it as difficult to think in an orderly way and following a plan as others who are well-educated try to follow a sermon without a plan. The preacher must be wise and careful in the preparation and preaching of his sermons to be suitable to the variety of hearers. It is possible to concentrate so much in producing an excellent plan that the real content and message of the passage is neglected.

4. The Preparation of the Main Divisions

The preparation of these divisions is not easy, but as they are so important we cannot be satisfied with our sermon until they are made. A number of things must be kept in mind when we are preparing these divisions.

4.1. Each division should bring a new thought

Each main division should help to give more information and expand your subject or text. While the divisions must be dealing directly with our subject, they must be entirely separate from each other. Each division should be complete in itself, that is, when you have finished with it nothing more needs to be added to explain that "thought" about the subject.

It is important that each main division is presenting a new thought about the subject or text. This means there can be no overlapping of what is in the divisions. Some preachers will say the same thing, but under a different heading, and think they are progressing with their sermon. This is not moving forward but staying in one place.

For example, a preacher may prepare a sermon on John 3:7 "You must be born again." His main points may be:

1.   What we mean by the new birth.
2.   Why we need the new birth.
3.   What the new birth will do for us.
4.   How we get the new birth.

Here it will be seen that the second and third divisions are overlapping and both mean the same thing.

If a preacher prepares a sermon on 1 Corinthians 2:14, "The natural person does not accept the things of the Spirit of God, for they are folly to him, and he is not able to understand them because they are spiritually discerned."

His main points may be:

1.   What Paul means by the natural man.
2.   Why the natural man does not accept the things of the Spirit of God.

3.   Why the natural man is not able to understand the things of the
      Spirit.

4.   Spiritual discernment is needed to understand the things of the
      Spirit.

Here it is clear that the third and fourth divisions are overlapping and
what the preacher says in one will be repeated in the other.

On the other hand, a preacher must not only give a new thought
in each division but he must keep to his theme. If a preacher prepares a
sermon on John 3:16 "For God so loved the world that He gave His only
Son, that whoever believes in Him should not perish but have eternal
life."

His main points may be:

1.   The great love of God - "*So loved*"

2.   The sacrificial love of God - "*Gave His only Son*"

3.   The rescuing love of God - "*Not perish*"

4.   The gift of God - "*Everlasting life*"

Here it is clear the preacher is having a theme on, "The love of God," as
the first, second and third points show. Therefore, the fourth point is
out of place even though it is a new thought and is found in the text. He
should have "the climax of the love of God" – "have eternal life."

Again if a preacher prepares a sermon on Ephesians 2:8-9 "For
by grace you have been saved through faith; and this is not your own
doing, it is the gift of God – not a result of works, so that no one may
boast."

His main points may be:

1.   The means of Salvation - *"By Grace"*

2.   The sinner is chosen by grace - *"By Grace"*

3.   The condition of Salvation - *"Through faith"*

4.   Human effort cannot help us get Salvation - *"Not of your own doing...not because of works"*

5.   The gift of Salvation - *"Gift of God"*

Here the preacher is having as his theme, "Salvation is the gift of God," as the divisions, one, three, four and five show. However, the second division, although found in the text, is not directly connected with this theme and should not be there. It could be used with another theme or topic dealing with "Grace."

Each division must present a new thought entirely distinct from the other divisions; but also a new thought in agreement with the theme for that sermon.

4.2. The divisions should show progression and order

The preacher may divide up his sermon into divisions but could still be wandering around in circles. He may say much in each division or section of his sermon but he is not going anywhere. Can you imagine some boys playing football without having goal posts at both ends of the compound? They just play with the ball back and forward and around in circles. However, if they want to be serious about the football game they will have goal posts and have two teams and each player in the team kicks the ball with the aim of going forward towards the goal posts and winning the game.

The preacher uses his divisions with the aim of going to the climax of his sermon. Therefore, the divisions should be in order, going forward step by step to the goal that is in mind for that sermon.

4.3. The divisions should come naturally

The important thing is that the divisions or points must be in the text and are the natural questions or sections found in it. If the text naturally falls into three sections it should not be forced to make four or five. If the text only divides into two parts, then do not get another one or two points from another place in the Bible and add them to the sermon of the text being considered. This means those extra points do not come from the text and should not be in the sermon.

If the text does not clearly say something, we do not read another thing into it or add what we think it says or what someone says about it. The points must come clearly from the text; there is no place for our own ideas or those of others. The truth we preach must be the Truth from the Word of God.

4.4. The number of divisions vary

There is no rule on the number of divisions a sermon should have. This depends very much on the text and the way you decide to treat it. We must remember why the divisions are there – to help the preacher and the hearer. It may be argued then that two divisions are not enough, as too much material would be in each section, and it would be difficult for both the preacher and the hearer to remember all that they contain. On the other hand, seven or eight divisions would be too many, as it could cause confusion and make it difficult to remember all of them.

5. The Preparation of the Sub-Divisions

What has been said about the main divisions can also be said about the sub-divisions. That is, they should:

a.   Bring a new thought.

b.   Show progression and order.

c.   Should come naturally.

d.   The number will vary.

These sub-divisions are important, as they help to break down the main points or headings of the sermon into smaller sections. Sometimes we may know what we want to say but cannot work out how to say it. Then we must take great care and not be in a hurry – this is why we need to start preparing the sermon in good time. Sometimes we may have to return to the sermon the next day, and again the following day, before we are finally able to divide it up.

The sub-divisions help the preacher explain his main section in an orderly and clear way. He is not wandering around in circles, but by dividing it up the hearer is able to understand what the preacher is saying.

6. The Use of Commentaries

Now it is time to look at commentaries and other books to check what we have done. It is important that we do not read commentaries to get our outline, but that we get it through prayer and meditation of the Scriptures. The use of commentaries too early in our preparation will restrict our thoughts, and make us concentrate on what they say.

We have already looked at Commentaries, Dictionaries, Handbooks, Concordances and other useful books to get the exact meaning of the words, the circumstances and details of the writings and events. This enables us to get all the information necessary to be accurate and informative in all details, but not to restrict our thoughts in the preparation of the sermon.

Now after we have meditated on the text, and been guided by the Holy Spirit in the preparation of our outline, we turn to the commentaries. This helps to give us new materials that did not come to our mind; it confirms what we have done, and keeps us accurate in our statements.

Note of warning: We should not read what is written in a commentary and say, "This is true, this is good, this is the 'Word of God.'" We must always remember the words in a commentary are the words of man. It is his idea, it is his interpretation and it greatly depends on his beliefs and views on Scripture and doctrine what he will say. No commentary can say all that could be said about any text in the Bible, and we cannot preach what the commentary says and be satisfied with our sermon. Therefore, we must always remember that the best interpreter of Scripture is the Holy Spirit. Let the Scriptures interpret the Scriptures and we will not be led to say something that is not Scriptural and untrue.

Assignment:

1. Why is it good to briefly note your thoughts in any order as you start to prepare a sermon?
2. How would you answer someone who says he can preach a good sermon without all this preparation and spending time on an outline?
3. Do you consider it necessary to divide up a sermon into divisions? Explain their advantages and disadvantages.
4. Prepare the main points for a sermon on Acts 4:12, Mark 8:36 and John 1:12.

5.	When, and in what way should commentaries be used in the preparation of sermons?

LESSON 7

THE TEXTUAL SERMON

When a sermon is preached from a text then it is called a textual sermon. The text may be part of a verse or a complete verse or even two or three verses of Scripture.

In the textual sermon, the text provides the divisions. The preacher carefully examines the words of the text, and develops the outline from it. In this way, the outline is kept strictly to the text and does not proceed in a different direction. He looks at the natural divisions of the text and uses them to make the main divisions of the sermon.

For example, if he prepares a sermon outline from John 10:28, "I give them eternal life, and they will never perish, and no one will snatch them out of my hand," it will be seen where the divisions could be made.

It may be divided into four sections. Thus, And I / give them eternal life; / and they will never perish, / and no one will snatch them out of my hand.

The preacher may now prepare the main divisions of the outline.

1. **The Character of the Shepherd – "And I"**

    Here the preacher explains who the "I" is. It is Jesus Christ, the good shepherd. He gives details of the character of the Shepherd.

2.　**The Gift of the Shepherd** – "gives them eternal life"

　　The Shepherd gives His sheep "eternal life." It is not something to be worked for or bought. It is eternal life with Christ, and it is a gift.

3.　**The Security of the Shepherd** – "and they will never perish"

　　Here the preacher explains that someone who gets eternal life from the Shepherd will never perish. He has got security with Christ. It is everlasting security, he will never perish.

4.　**The Protection of the Shepherd**

　　The Shepherd protects His sheep. No one can pluck the sheep away. He is able to keep them and protect them. We have no need to fear anything for the Shepherd will never allow us to be taken out of His protecting hands.

The example above shows that the main divisions in a textual outline must be taken from the verse. Therefore, a preacher cannot take a text and then preach a sermon that is not closely linked to that text. From the above example the thought is, "The proclamation of the Good Shepherd." This thought is expanded under four main headings, which is the division of the text.

For another example let us look at Isaiah 45:22 "Turn to me / and be saved, / all the ends of the earth / for I am God and there is no other." The preacher may now prepare the main divisions of the outline e.g.

1.　**The one to whom we are to turn** – "Turn to me… for I am God and there is no other."

　　Many people want to turn from their sorrows and troubles, but do not know where they should turn. Here we are told to turn to God, for there is no other. No one can do more for us than God. He has created us and He sent Jesus Christ to take our sins so that we might be free.

2.   **The reason why we are to turn** – "And be saved"

When we turn to God He can do something for us. He can rescue and save us from our sins. He is the only one who can save us and there is no other way to be saved.

3.   **Everyone is called to turn** – "All the ends of the earth"

God does not confine his offer of salvation to a few. Everyone who turns to God will be saved. Everyone who looks to Jesus for pardon and cleansing will receive it. His offer is to "whosoever believeth" shall not perish.

For another example let us look at Philippians 4:4 "Rejoice / in the Lord /always; / again I will say rejoice."

1.   **The command given** – "Rejoice"

Few people today want to rejoice. They complain about the government; about the Church, about their work; about their friends. Nevertheless, here the Bible tells us to rejoice. When people are happy it makes others happy. Therefore, we should rejoice because we are commanded to do it and it is profitable to others and to ourselves.

2.   **The object of our rejoicing** – "In the Lord"

We should rejoice "in the Lord." This gives us great cause for rejoicing, as He is our Lord; Saviour; Redeemer and God. Let us rejoice and be glad in the Lord.

3.   **The time to rejoice** – "always"

When we have no cause for rejoicing because of our circumstances or feelings, we can still rejoice in the Lord. There is no time when we cannot rejoice in Him. When others are with you rejoice in the Lord. When you are alone, rejoice in the Lord.

4.   **The command is emphasized** – "Again I will say rejoice"
      Paul rejoiced in all his circumstances. The Christian is called upon to rejoice again and again. Don't just think about it once, but let it be a continuous attitude and desire of your heart.

For another example, let us look at Galatians 3:23. "Now before faith came, / we were held captive under the law, imprisoned / until the coming faith would be revealed."

1.   **The original condition** – "Before faith came"
      We do not have faith by nature. We want to live our own lives and through our own efforts look after ourselves. We did not understand the meaning or existence of faith. We may have seen it in others but never put it into practice in our own lives. We lived selfish lives, seeking only to please ourselves and believing faith had no part in us.

2.   **We were kept in bondage** – "we were held captive under the law, imprisoned"
      We tried to keep within the law of the Ten Commandments but the desire to sin was there. It was the law that restrained us from going deeper into sin. The law restrained our movements and actions. It showed us where we are wrong but it could do nothing to help deliver us from the bondage of Satan.

3.   **The revelation that gave us freedom** – "until the coming faith would be revealed"
      The only thing that could help us, and deliver us from our bondage is "faith." When it was revealed to us what faith is, then it set us free. Faith in Christ delivered us from the power of Satan. Without faith, it is not possible to please God. "Therefore being justified by faith, we have peace with God." Romans 5:1.

The following outlines show in more detail, the main divisions and sub-divisions of textual sermons. The preacher should take time to practise this method of making outlines from various texts. The work is difficult but the rewards are great both for the preacher and for the congregation.

TEXT: Matthew 11:28 "Come to me, / all who labour and are heavy laden, / and I will give / you rest."

THEME: Christ's invitation to heavenly rest.

Introduction

1. **The person who gives the invitation** - "Come to me"

    a.   It is Jesus Christ, the Son of God.

    b.   He has got all power and authority.

    c.   His invitation is reliable.

2. **To whom does he give the invitation** - "all who labour and are heavy laden"

    a.   All can come, no matter who they are.

    b.   Labouring to gain salvation will not help.

    c.   He wants those who are burdened.

3. **The assurance of the invitation** - "and I will give"

    a.   He *will* give - there is no doubt.

    b.   He has all power behind His promise.

4. **The result of the invitation guaranteed** - "you rest"

    a.   Rest of heart; rest of conscience; rest of mind

    b.   Eternal rest in heaven.

Conclusion:

TEXT: Acts 8: 4 "Now those who were scattered / went about/ preaching the word"

THEME: Witnessing for Christ.

Introduction:

1. **Who preached?** – "those who were scattered"

    a.   Was it the Apostles only?

    b.   It was the ordinary believers.

2. **What did they preach?** – "preaching the Word"

    a.   Did they preach politics about the Roman government?

    b.   It was the Word of God.

    c.   The birth, death and resurrection of Christ.

3. **Why did they preach?**

    a.   They believed the Word of God. – 2 Corinthians 4:13.

    b.   They believed the men were perishing.

    c.   They were commanded to do it by Jesus – Matt. 28:19.

4. **Where did they preach?** – "Went about"

    a.   Not only in Synagogues and churches.

    b.   They preached and witnessed everywhere.

Conclusion:

TEXT: Ephesians 2:8 "By grace / you / have been saved / though faith"

THEME: The wonder of our Salvation.

Introduction:

1. **The means of salvation** - "By Grace"

    a.   Explanation of the meaning of grace.

    b.   Difference between grace and law – John 1:17.

    c.   Connection between grace and Salvation – Titus 2:11-14.

2. **Those who are saved** – "you"

    a.   Those dead through trespasses and sins v. 1.

    b.   Those following this world v. 2.

    c.   Those who lived in the passions of the flesh v. 3.

3. **There is no doubt about the salvation** – "have been saved"

    a.   Today many people are not sure of their salvation.

    b.   However there can be do doubt. We *have been,* and are *going to be* or *hope to be,* saved.

4. **How they were saved** - "though faith"

    a.   We are saved by grace.

    b.   Through faith.

Conclusion:

Assignment:

1. What is meant by text?
2. What are the advantages and disadvantages of a text?
3. How is a sermon outline made from a text?
4. Can someone prepare a sermon and then look for a Bible reading and text that is suitable for it?
5. Make a sermon outline from John 3:16 and Luke 9:25.

THE EXPOSITORY SERMON

The expository sermon is the best and most effective means of preaching and teaching the Word of God. The textual sermon is usually confined to a verse of Scripture and the thought that it teaches; whereas the expository sermon examines a large portion of scripture and is an exposition of it. An exposition takes one theme or central thought of a portion of Scripture and then explains and expounds it. It is not a series of comments about each verse in the passage, so the preacher needs to be careful he does not fall into this error.

1. The advantages of the expository sermon

Preachers often neglect this type of preaching. They claim that this type of sermon is too difficult to make and would rather preach the textual sermon. However, there are many advantages in expository preaching for both the preacher and the congregation.

1.1. Expository preaching gives a greater knowledge of the Scriptures

As a portion of Scripture is taken and expounded, both the preacher and the hearer come to have a greater knowledge and understanding of the Scriptures. Each portion of Scripture is studied as part of the whole

Bible. The message is based on the Scriptures and it has the authority of God.

Where a preacher and congregation study the Scriptures in this way they will be richly rewarded. Both will grow spiritually and will be instructed in the Word of God.

1.2. Expository preaching enables the preacher to deal with personal matters

If a preacher is giving an exposition of a chapter or book of the Bible, he could speak with confidence about some matters that could cause embarrassment if he was to deal with them as a topic or textual sermon.

For example, if he is giving an exposition of Matthew chapter 5, he will be speaking about many blessings as found in the first eleven verses. Another sermon will be expounding how we are the salt of the earth and the light of the world. Other sermons will deal with murder, adultery, swearing falsely, love of enemies and divorce. No one can accuse the preacher of preaching at them if he is expounding the Scriptures according to a plan.

1.3. Expository preaching prevents the preacher from always speaking on his favourite subject

It can become easy for a preacher to have his favourite subjects and texts, and almost every sermon with this thought in mind. This means there are many other truths from the Scriptures that are being neglected.

Expository preaching forces the preacher to speak about other matters and enables him to have new material for every sermon. An expository preacher cannot say the same thing week after week. He has to prepare and research the material for every sermon. The preacher and the congregation will benefit greatly by this experience.

Although expository preaching is the best and most effective means of preaching and teaching the Word of God, there are disadvantages and things to be avoided if it is to be successful.

1. Expository preaching will fail if it becomes a series of comments on the verses

An expository sermon that is not properly prepared as a complete thought on the total verses chosen as the text, will fail. It could easily become a collection of small sermons or comments on each verse. The preacher can have four or five verses as his text and for thirty minutes give comments on each verse and at the conclusion think he had been successful in preaching a good expository sermon.

Great care must be taken in the preparation of the sermon and it involves a lot of hard work. The lazy preacher will just comment on the verses chosen, but the serious and honest preacher will prepare his sermon thoroughly.

2. Expository preaching could cause people to stay away from church

If the preacher makes his sermons full of facts and details that the congregation is not able to understand; or he makes his preaching so uninteresting that the hearer becomes weary he has failed. It has been known for preachers to expound a book of the Bible that lasts for weeks and months and be so dull and uninteresting that some members will stay away until he finishes the book.

All preaching must be interesting and relevant to the present needs of the congregation. Expository preaching can do that if the preacher is aware of the dangers and makes a determined effort to be successful.

2. The Preparation of the Expository Sermon

The preacher selects the passage to be expounded, taking into consideration what we studied in lesson 3 about the selection of the text. After a careful reading and studying the passage the main thought or theme is considered. There may be more than one "thought" in the passage, so the one that is going to be developed should be chosen, and written down.

After the theme is chosen then the main thoughts contributing to that theme are selected. These are arranged in order and the sub-divisions inserted to complete the outline.

Now let us look at 1 John 4:7-12 and see how we can make a rough outline with the main headings.

The theme for the passage is "The love of God and the love of ourselves."

1.   **God is love - v. 8**

Here it is seen that God is love. This is one of His attributes. It is His nature to love. God has shown the meaning of true sacrificial love. He does not count the cost, but gives freely.

2.   **God has shown His love - vs. 9 and 10**

God has shown His love in a visible way. He sent His Son into the world. It is through His Son we have eternal life for He is our atoning sacrifice.

3.   **Our love comes from God – vs. 7, 11 and 12**

Love does not exist apart from God, because it comes from God. Where God is, there is love, and where God is not, there is hate. Where there is true sacrificial love in a person then that person knows God for he has been given that love by God.

For another example, look at Romans 5:1-5

The theme for the passage is "peace and joy in Christ."

1. **The source of peace – vs. 1 and 2a**

    We were dead in our sins but through faith in the Lord Jesus Christ we have been justified. We rejected God but now we have peace with God. We were separated from God but we have access through faith into this grace in which we now possess.

2. **The object of our joy – vs. 2b, 3 and 4**

    Not only do we have peace with God but we also rejoice in the hope of the glory of God. We should also rejoice when we are in suffering for this tests us and proves how genuine is our faith. By our sufferings, we mature in the Christian life.

3. **The reason for our peace and joy – v. 5**

    God has poured His love into our hearts. Therefore, the hope of the coming glory will not be a disappointment. This is why we can have peace because we know all is well with us for eternity. This happy situation makes us to rejoice.

Now we will use Titus 3:3-8 to give an outline of the divisions and sub-divisions. Here our text tells us to speak evil of no man, but to do that which is good. Therefore, the theme of the passage is "the doing of good works."

As we carefully read the passage, we see that Paul is referring to the past and the condition that we once were in. This could be explained under the heading, "Our past condition."

Then he explained what Jesus Christ has done for us and we could explain this under the heading, "what has been done for us." Finally, he shows that for the believer he should be doing what is good. The heading to explain this may be, "Carefully maintain good works."

We are now ready to write the main points of the outline as we have stated.

1.   Our past condition - *verse 3*
2.   What has been done for us - *verses 4-7*
3.   Carefully maintain good works - *verse 8*

We need to examine each division more closely and find out more details. It will be seen that we can have a number of sub-divisions in each main division, as follows:

1.   Our past condition - *v.3*
     a.   Foolish, disobedient and deceived
     b.   Slaves of passions and pleasures and hating one another
2.   What has been done for us – *vs. 4-7*
     a.   Our Saviour appeared
     b.   He saved us
3.   Carefully maintain good works – *v.8*
     a.   Because you have trusted God
     b.   It is the natural response
     c.   It is profitable for everyone

For another example, let us look at John 20:10-18. Here we have an account of Jesus appearing to Mary Magdalene. Perhaps as our theme, we could say, "Mary is seeking for Jesus." From the previous verses, we know that Peter and another disciple find the empty tomb. As they did not find Jesus and could not understand what has happened they went back home. However, Mary remained outside the tomb. Here Mary was trying in her own way to find Jesus. This could be explained under the heading, "A soul seeking Jesus tries its own way."

Later we see that Mary meets the angels but is not surprised by such strange things. She seemed to think it nothing strange. This could be explained under the heading, "A soul seeking Jesus is not interested in anything else." Finally, we see that Mary is standing beside Jesus and she does not know it. This can be explained under the heading, "A soul seeking Jesus may not know when He is very near." Now she has found Jesus and her joy is complete. Therefore, "the seeking soul will find Jesus."

Now the main divisions may be written down:

1. A soul seeking Jesus tried its own ways – *verses 10, 11 and 15b*.
2. A soul seeking Jesus is not interested in anything else – *verse 12 and 13.*
3. A soul seeking Jesus may not know when He is very near – *verses 14 and 15.*
4. The seeking soul will find Jesus – *verse 16-18.*

As the passage is studied more details can be added to give a complete outline. e.g.

1. **A soul seeking Jesus tries its own way** – *vs. 10, 11 and 15b*
   a. She stayed at the tomb when others had left
   b. She looked inside and searched the tomb
   c. She asked the "gardener" where He was so that she could see Him
2. **A soul seeking Jesus is not interested in anything else** – *vs. 12-13*
   a. She was not astonished when she saw the angels
   b. She does not have time for a general conversation with the "gardener"
3. **A soul seeking Jesus may not know when he is very near** – *vs. 12-13*
   a. Jesus was beside her but she did not know it.

    b.   Jesus spoke to her but she was not aware of it.

4.   A soul seeking Jesus will find Him

    a.   Jesus called her personally by name, and she believed

    b.   She immediately began to witness of Jesus

For another example of an expository sermon outline, look at 1 Peter 1:3-5. As we read and study this passage we see the Apostle Peter is writing of the great hope the Christian has of an eternal inheritance in heaven.

In verse 3, the Apostle is speaking of the great mercy of God. It is through God and the mercy of God, the Christian receives his new life. Therefore, the verse shows how the Christian receives a new birth.

Verse 4 gives details of the inheritance the new believer receives and verse 5 explains that it is through God's power that we are kept until the coming of the salvation that is ready to be revealed in the last time.

The main points of the outline can now be written down:

1.   The new birth of the Christian
2.   The inheritance of the Christian
3.   The guardian of the Christian

Now if we examine these divisions more closely we will be able to develop the outline. The Apostle praises God for His great mercy in giving the Christian a new birth. It is a living hope through the resurrection of Jesus Christ. Therefore, the sub-divisions may be; (a) it is something to praise God about (b) It is a living hope.

The second division speaks of the inheritance that can never perish; it will not spoil or fade; it is kept in heaven for the Christian. We may use this as the sub-division; (a) It will never perish (b) it will not spoil or fade (c) it is kept in heaven for the Christian.

The third division may be explained by showing that it is through faith the Christian is guarded by God's power. The just shall live by faith. His salvation will be kept safe ready to be revealed in the last day. So the sub-divisions may be: (a) The Christian puts his faith in God (b) He is kept by God's power.

The complete outline may be:

1. **The new birth of the Christian** – *verse 3*

    a.   It is something to give praise for

    b.   It is a living hope

2. **The inheritance of the Christian** – *verse 4*

    a.   It will never perish

    b.   It will not spoil or fade

    c.   It is kept in heaven for him

3. **The guardian of the Christian** – *verse 5*

    a.   He puts his faith in God

    b.   He is kept by God's power

The young preacher may believe he could never make an outline for an expository sermon but if he works hard and has constant practice he will be able to do it. We only need to study these outlines to see the great values to both the preacher and the hearer that this type of preaching brings.

Therefore, to start with, the preacher should not attempt chapters or books of the Bible but try a few easy passages. Try the following and you will be surprised how successful you can be. John 1:29-34; John 14:5-14; Romans 3:21-31; Romans 5:1-11; Galatians 5:1-12; Ephesians 2:1-10; Philemon 4:7; and James 5:7-12.

Assignment:

1. What do we mean by an expository sermon?
2. What are the advantages of expository preaching?
3. What are the dangers to be avoided in an expository sermon?
4. How does someone start to prepare an expository sermon?
5. Prepare the outline of an expository sermon on Colossians 1:15-20.

THE TOPICAL SERMON

A topical sermon is one in which a topic or subject is chosen and then the divisions are derived from the subject to explain it. In preparing the sermon, the preacher starts with the topic he is led to speak about, and then searches the Scriptures to get information to explain it.

This means that the topical sermon does not need a text to start with, as the Bible must be used to explain it. The main divisions must be taken from the topic and these are supported by the Scriptures.

To understand this more clearly, let us select a topic and prepare a topical outline. Take for example the topic of *Prayer.*

1. **What is prayer**
    a.   Adoration – Psalm 95:6
    b.   Confession – Psalm 32:5
    c.   Thanksgiving – Philippians 4:6
    d.   Supplication – Timothy 2:1
2. **Where to pray**
    a.   Everywhere – Timothy 2:8
    b.   In Secret – Matthew 6:6
    c.   In the Temple (Church) – Luke 18:10
    d.   Private prayer, family, public prayer

3. **When to pray**

    a.   Always – Luke 18:1, 1 Thessalonians 5:17

    b.   In the morning – Psalm 5:3

    c.   At noon and in the evening – Psalm 55:17

    d.   Daily – Psalm 86:3

4. **Subjects for prayer**

    a.   For the sick – James 5:13-16

    b.   For all men and all in authority – 1 Timothy 2:1-4

    c.   For personal safety – Daniel 6:18-23

    d.   For wisdom – 1 Kings 3:5-9

    e.   For those who persecute you – Matthew 5:38-48

It will be seen from the above outline that we have not confined ourselves to one portion of the Scriptures. We have examined prayer under four divisions and used many references in the Bible to explain them. Much more could be said about the subject, such as; conditions for prayer; hindrances to prayer; how to pray and the result of prayer, but it would be too much for one sermon. This subject is so big it would take a number of sermons to touch each aspect of it.

To ask questions about the topic or subject is an effective way of explaining all about it. For example, if we take the topic or subject *Faith,* we can ask a series of questions to give a full knowledge of the subject.

1. **What** is Faith?

    Here the word Faith is explained, so that everyone understands exactly what it is.

2. **Why** do we need Faith?

    Here it can be explained why this subject has been chosen and why it is necessary for everyone to have Faith.

3.   **How** do we get Faith?

Is it something we buy or how do we get it? The answer to this question explains the circumstances under which Faith is received.

4.   **Who** gets Faith or **What** is the object of Faith?

Here it is explained who gets Faith or receives it. We must put our Faith in a trust-worthy person.

5.   **Where** does Faith come from?

The answer to this question may help many anxious hearts on where they can receive this Faith.

6.   **When** do we get Faith?

Again some hearer may be concerned about when he may receive Faith; and this division will answer the question.

7.   **The results** of Faith.

In conclusion, the hearer wants to know what are the results of having Faith. This can be made known.

Clearly not all of these questions will be used in every sermon. However, it can be a very effective way of studying in depth any topic or subject. The Bible is searched to find the answers to these questions.

Let us now put this into practice for another sermon outline. We will have the topic *The New Birth*.

1.   **What do we mean by being born again?**

a.   Nicodemus asked this question – John 3:4

b.   It is a spiritual birth – John 3:8

2.   **Why do we need to be born again?**

a.   In the beginning Adam and Eve sinned – Genesis 3

b.   All have sinned – Romans 3:23

c.   Without a new birth we cannot see heaven – John 3:3

3. **Who needs to be born again?**
    a. Nicodemus the religious teacher – John 3:7
    b. Paul the chief of sinners – Timothy 1:15
    c. All need to be born again – Romans 3:10

4. **How are we born again?**
    a. Acknowledge that you are a sinner – Romans 5:1
    b. Believe on the Lord Jesus Christ – Romans 5:8
    c. Commit yourself to Christ who went to the cross – John 1:12

5. **What are the results of being born again?**
    a. Peace with God – Romans 5:1
    b. Peace of conscience – Philippians 3:7
    c. A new creation – 2 Corinthians 5:17
    d. Assurance of eternal life – Romans 6:23

For another example let us consider the topic, *Forgiveness.*

1. **The Author of Forgiveness**
    a. Jesus forgives sins – Luke 7:48-50
    b. God forgives sins – Mark 2:7

2. **The Means of Forgiveness**
    a. On the grounds of the Lord's compassion – Psalm 78:39
    b. On the grounds of divine justice – 1 John 1:9
    c. On the blood of Christ – Ephesians 1:7

3. **The Conditions of Forgiveness**
    a. Repentance – Acts 5:31
    b. Faith – Luke 7:50
    c. Confession – 1 John 1:9
    d. Fogiving others – Matthew 6:15

4. **The Conditions for Forgiveness**
    a. All sins are forgiven – Luke 7:47

b. All trespasses forgiven (Not one sin remains unforgiven) – Colossians 2:13

The topical sermon is a very effective way of understanding a topic or subject and what the Bible as a whole teaches concerning it. The doctrines of the Bible can be studied in this way, by using material and facts throughout the Bible.

For the preacher who is preparing such a sermon he has much studying and searching through the Bible to get all the information on the subject. He cannot use this type of preaching every Sunday or he will reach a place he can no longer think of a new topic or subject to preach on. He will also find it difficult doing all the preparation needed to treat the subject in full.

Assignment:

1. What is the difference between a topical sermon and an expository sermon?
2. How does someone prepare a topical sermon?
3. What are the advantages and disadvantages of a topical sermon?
4. Prepare an outline on the "The love of Jesus."
5. Prepare an outline on "The hope of the believers."

LESSON 10

THE INTRODUCTION

"You will find the word that I have chosen as my text in the portion of the Scripture that we have just read…," is the way that many preachers week after week begin their sermons. Another way they start their sermons is to say, "Today the theme of my sermon is…" This may be acceptable occasionally but it certainly would not be good to begin sermons every Sunday with such a statement. If we do, we will lose the attention of our audience before we even begin. We are not giving them anything interesting to make them start to listen to what we have to say.

The introduction is a very important part of the sermon. If we fail in our introduction, it makes a bad start, and may make the complete sermon a failure. Great care and patience must be taken in the preparation of the introduction.

1. Prepare the introduction last

There are many good reasons why the introduction should be prepared after the sermon.

a. Until the theme of the sermon we are going to develop is known, and the material being used, we cannot know the best way to introduce it. If we start preparing the sermon with the introduction, we may find that as the sermon develops our introduction is not suitable. The sermon may now, be different from what we had first thought.

b.   An introduction prepared first can be too long. It is only after the sermon has been prepared, then we can prepare a short, clear and relevant introduction to it.

c.   When starting to prepare a sermon our minds are full of many things we want to say about the text. If we start with our introduction many of these thoughts will be put into it, which should be at various places throughout the sermon.

2. The purpose of the introduction

The introduction to a sermon has many important functions. It is good if the preacher thinks carefully about these when he prepares his sermons. No one starts to talk to a stranger without a few words of greeting and introduction. In the same way, no preacher can enter into the discussion or body of his sermon without an introduction. If the stranger we meet impresses us with a good introduction we will listen carefully to what he has to say. However, if his introduction is not interesting, if his manner is not good, if his speech is not clear, if his behaviour is not right, we will not want to listen to what he has to say. The same lessons apply to the preacher if he wants the congregation to listen to his sermon.

2.1. The introduction should be interesting

The introduction should make the hearer interested in what the preacher is going to preach about. We cannot take for granted that every member of the congregation is sitting up with great interest for the sermon. Therefore, the first few moments of the sermon are very important. In that time the preacher can raise the interest of the hearer so that he wants to hear more, or he can cause the hearer to lose interest and his mind and thoughts start to wander to other things.

An introduction that does not make the hearer interested in what the preacher is saying, will result in the preacher having no hearer as he enters his discussion or body of the sermon. The introduction should be something to make the hearer take an interest in what is being said, and want to hear more.

2.2. The introduction should be varied

One way of making the introductions interesting is to have them varied. To always begin each sermon in the same way week after week does nothing to help the hearer who wants to listen to the sermon. After the singing of the hymn before the sermon, many people settle down and let their thoughts go aimlessly until the sermon is finished, because, the preacher always begins his sermons the same way and there is nothing to arrest attention.

There are many methods the preacher can use to help vary his introduction:

a. **From the text.** An interesting introduction may be given by explaining the circumstances of the text in the light of the context. Sometimes it is necessary to explain why a thing was said or written; why some people take the wrong meaning from the text or why the writer used certain words and what these words mean in other places in the Bible.

b. **From the context or book.** Sometimes it is necessary to examine the context to get the meaning of the text and this explanation can be your introduction. It introduces what you are going to say later and why you are going to say it. It explains the events that caused the text to be written.

c.   **From the historical setting or customs of the people.** Sometimes an interesting introduction may be given by describing the political, religious and social situation of the country when the events we are considering took place. On occasions, we may have to explain the culture and customs of the people. This is all necessary for the hearer to understand the circumstances that surround the text and it becomes more meaningful to him.

When considering the "Good Samaritan" we need to explain why the Jews and Samaritans had no dealings with one another. Jerusalem is about 2,500 feet above sea level and Jericho is about 1,000 feet below sea level, so going 'down' from Jerusalem to Jericho has more meaning when this is explained.

When we know the custom of a servant washing the feet of strangers to refresh them after walking on sandy roads, we understand the position Jesus took when he washed the disciples' feet, as no servant had done it.

When we know how the Israelites were under the Persian government and the condition of Jerusalem after its destruction we understand better the position of Haggai, Zechariah or Nehemiah.

d.   **By asking a question.** A sermon can be introduced by the asking of a challenging question to arouse the interest of the hearer. He wants to hear more; to hear how the preacher is going to answer that one, or perhaps it is the question that he would ask, and he is anxious to hear more.

e.   **By using an interesting story or illustration.** This is not the time to give a long detailed story that will take 5 or 10 minutes, rather a short – to the point story that will lead into the body of the sermon. Therefore, the story or illustration must be relevant to the theme and must be suitable to introduce the thought that we are taking from the text.

f. **By using a surprising statement.** A sermon can be introduced by saying something that causes the hearer to be surprised. This is the method sometimes used by the prophets and by Jesus Christ. They made a surprising statement that caused the people to be interested in what they were saying. Great care must be taken when this kind of introduction is used, so that we do not raise the interest of the hearer and are not able to maintain it throughout the sermon. A surprising statement can fall flat if we are not able to use it in a meaningful way as we continue into the sermon. However, if properly used it is an excellent way to begin the sermon and much more meaningful and exciting than to begin with the words, "Today the theme for my message is …"

2.3. The introduction should be short

It has been known for preachers to have a very long introduction and a short sermon. This happens mostly when he is preaching a series of sermons from a chapter or book of the Bible. His introduction consists of a summary of what he preached the Sunday before about the verses preceding those that he is now going to consider. To give a long introduction like this is tiresome especially for those who faithfully attend Church every Sunday, and were present the week before to hear the complete sermon.

The introduction should be short, raise the interest of the hearer and give him the desire to hear more. Neither part of last week's sermon nor of the present sermon should be included in the introduction. If a story is used, or details of the customs of the people, or explanation of the context of the text, then it must be short and interesting, leading into the body of the sermon.

2.4. The introduction should be definite

Some preachers begin their sermons with an apology. "I should not be here today as many in this congregation are better qualified than myself to speak…," "I'm sorry my time is very short so this sermon will have to be brief…," "I was very busy this week so I didn't have time to prepare this sermon as well as I would like…" This is an entirely wrong way to start a sermon. The preacher is raising attention to himself and not to the text and the Word of God.

Where the preacher is trying to get sympathy for himself, if he tries to show that he is well educated and superior to the majority in the congregation, he is drawing attention to himself rather than Christ. There is no place in the pulpit for an apology or pride. Instead draw your hearers to Christ and let your introduction be the beginning of that process.

Assignment:

1. What is the purpose of the introduction?
2. When should the introduction for a sermon be prepared?
3. What are the qualifications of a good introduction?
4. Listen to three sermons and see if the introductions are good.
5. How can the introduction be varied week by week?

LESSON 11

THE CONCLUSION

When an experienced driver teaches someone how to drive a motor car, he not only explains how to start the car and move forward, but also how to stop. Knowing how to apply the brakes and stop the car is as important if not more important, as knowing how to start. When driving a car you do all that is necessary to start, then you travel along smoothly, and finally you slow down and stop. A complete sermon is like this. You do all that is necessary to start, that is the introduction; then you go along smoothly, that is the body or discussion of the sermon, and finally you slow down and stop, that is the conclusion.

A person will take his car when he has a purpose for going to a place, and when he reaches his destination he stops. Every sermon should have a purpose and destination and when that place is reached, the preacher should stop. You can picture the disaster that would take place when a driver doesn't know how to stop his vehicle. It is equally disastrous for a preacher who does not know how to stop his sermon.

The conclusion is not just stopping but declaring clearly and strongly, and bringing to a definite end and climax, that which has been explained and expounded in the body of the sermon. Many good sermons have been ruined by bad conclusions. Preachers carefully prepare the introduction and body of their sermon but leave the conclusion unfinished, believing that when the time comes, and they are preaching the sermon, they will know how to conclude it.

Because the conclusion is the climax of the whole sermon, and it brings the hearers to the point of making a commitment or response to the teaching of the Word of God, the preacher should give the greatest care and preparation to what he will say in these decisive moments.

1. The conclusion should not contain new material

The conclusion is not the time to bring in a new thought or say something that was forgotten earlier in the body of the sermon. This could suddenly distract the minds of the hearer as we approach the most important part of the sermon.

In a well-prepared sermon there should be nothing left out. The preparation of the division and sub-divisions will cover everything that needs to be said. If, however, a new thought does come to the mind of the preacher at the end of his sermon it should not be expressed but leave it for another occasion.

2. The conclusion should not be long

The conclusion that is long and drawn out makes the hearer restless and weary. Nothing can do more damage to a sermon than a conclusion that goes on and on with the appearance of no end. The preacher, who says "finally" or "in conclusion" and then continues on for some time, spoils the effect of his whole sermon. The hearer at this point may cease to listen even though the preacher continues.

A preacher should never refer to the time. Many preachers begin their conclusion by saying, "As my time is up, let me conclude by saying…" Again this distracts the hearer from the message and now becomes conscious of the time and waits for the preacher to stop speaking. The preacher has effectively lost his audience.

Therefore, in the conclusion do not say or do anything to cause the hearer to think about anything other than the very important issues now before him. The conclusion should be short (but not too short) with a powerful expression or statement that stops the sermon at the climax.

3. The conclusion should be personal

While it may be acceptable throughout the body of the sermon to speak in general terms, this cannot be done in the conclusion. It is now time to be personal. It is time to apply the great truths of the Word of God to the individual.

When the preacher ends his sermon by speaking in terms of "They…" "Those people…," "a person should…," he is not making the individual listener apply what is being said to himself, but dismisses it as something for the other person.

Great preachers, who have been effective in their ministry, are those who have been able to speak to hundreds or thousands of people in a gathering, as though they were talking to a friend. If a person can sit in a large congregation of people and hear the preacher talking as if he were the only person present, then he will be forced to think and act on what he has heard.

The prophet Amos started his message by condemning and attacking the sins of the enemies of Israel, but then he moved closer to attack Judah and finally Israel herself. When the prophet was speaking against the enemies of Israel the people were happy to hear the message, but when he condemned the personal sins of Israel he got a response, and the hearers were forced to consider their own sin and condition before God.

The effective preacher must conclude his sermon by applying the teaching of the Word of God to the personal needs of the hearer.

4. The conclusion should be varied

Just as the introduction to the sermon should vary, so also should the conclusion. A person, who faithfully attends his church week after week where the preacher always concludes his sermons in the same way, knows when the end is coming, and from that point has stopped listening. He looks for his hymnbook and gets it ready for the closing hymn that will soon be announced.

To avoid this type of thing happening, the preacher must vary his conclusions so that the regular hearer does not stop listening at the climax and most important point of the sermon.

The following methods may be used to give variety in conclusion.

a. **A brief summary of the main points.** This is not the opportunity to preach another sermon or add new material to what you have already said. Rather, by reminding the hearer of your arguments, or the progression of the discussion, you are able to re-emphasize and bring all that has been said to the climax point.

   Therefore, it is better not to use the exact words but use well-chosen statements that express the thought you had in each main division. By doing this you are able very quickly to recap what you have said over the past 30 minutes and the hearer is reminded of your main points and now it all joins together to come to the conclusion. That conclusion you have reached, is now plain before them and they are expected to act upon it.

b. **An illustration.** Sometimes the truths that you are trying to present in the sermon can be clearly and powerfully brought home to the hearer by an illustration. The illustration should be brief and told in such a way that it will conclude the sermon without any additional words or explanation.

Since the conclusion is the climax to your sermon, you must be very careful that the illustration serves this purpose, and is not a distraction or anti-climax to the theme of your message.

c.   **A Prayer.** Sometimes after the discussion and gradual ascending to a climax, the only thing that brings it to a conclusion is to pray. This prayer should not be a summary of the sermon or a sermonette in itself. It should be an earnest and honest petition that is the natural conclusion to the message of the sermon.

Too often this prayer has been used as an appeal to the emotions of the hearers. The preacher pleads in his prayer for the people to respond to the message, or the great disaster that will come upon them it they fail to do so. This is not a climax and conclusion to the sermon but a dishonest and irreverent attitude to prayer.

When a response to the sermon leads to a committing of oneself to the Lord and to His work then it can be expressed in a sincere prayer.

d.   **The text.** When the theme of the message and the divisions that were used to explain and expand it came from the text, then a suitable conclusion may be to quote the text itself.

A preacher may take as his text, Joshua 24:15 "Choose this day whom you will serve..." After expounding the Word of God and presenting the challenge and responsibility to the hearer of deciding for God, a fitting conclusion is a forceful repetition of the text, "Choose this day whom you will serve... as for me and my house, we will serve the Lord."

e.   **An application or appeal.** Quite often the application runs throughout the sermon and is not something only for the last three minutes. However, there is still the opportunity of making a final application to the truths contained in the message. When the sermon demands a response on the part of the hearer then the only conclusion we can come to, is to apply that truth to our own lives.

The preacher may appeal to his hearers in the way that Joshua appealed to the children of Israel. It is not an emotional appeal but a call to obedience on the part of the hearer to the Word of God. Through this personal appeal it is made clear that something is expected of the individual who hears the message, and he should respond to it, and apply it to his life.

Assignment:

1. Why is it important to prepare a good conclusion?
2. What are the qualifications of a good conclusion?
3. Why should the conclusion be varied?
4. How can the conclusion be varied?
5. Listen to three sermons and see if the conclusions meet the conditions of a good conclusion.

LESSON 12

THE APPLICATION

The application should not be confused with the conclusion. Mostly the conclusion is an application but the two are not the same. The application is applying the truth of the message to the personal needs of the hearer, whereas the conclusion is bringing the message to a close.

1. Applying the truth to the needs and problems of the hearer

A preacher may preach an excellent sermon, give a correct interpretation of the text, and yet the hearer leave the service unconvinced that the message had anything to do with him personally. Many people attend church with fears and problems and they are seeking for an answer. Therefore, the preacher has a duty of not only preaching a Biblical message but also applying that message to the present day situation.

The preacher must be a man who has knowledge and experience of the problems that the ordinary person faces. Sometimes preachers are accused of being distant from the reality of life. Their sermons are made in their study and are an accurate exposition of the Word of God but they are unable to apply it to the conditions of the hearer. They do not help the people who are facing the problems of guilt, hatred, envy, anger, loneliness, and many other needs in the society today. Therefore, the preacher must seek to apply the truth he is preaching to his people.

2. Make the application specific

A preacher can make his application general. This is better than no application, but it is much better if it can be pointed and specific. People today are saying, "I have a great problem, what should I do? Can you help me?" The answer to this cry for help cannot be given in general terms. It is a definite need and it requires definite help and advice.

The preacher can give a specific and clear application without making it obvious that he is speaking directly to a certain individual in the congregation. A preacher must never refer to an individual, or what some one has told him in confidence, when making his application.

3. The time in the sermon to make the application

Some preachers will make the application only at the end of the sermon. When doing so they will speak to both the Christian and the unconverted in every sermon, but every sermon should not end in an application to both types of people. An application to the believers will also challenge the unbeliever by the Spirit of God. It is always profitable to make an application at the end of the sermon, but there are many good opportunities throughout the sermon to apply the truth that is being taught. If the sermon is an exposition of the Word of God then it is wise to make the application at various opportune times as it progresses. This may mean there is an application at each division throughout the sermon. To leave it all to the end would be meaningless and unsuitable.

4. The application should carry conviction

A preacher may be able to expound the Word of God and give an application to its meaning, but be unable to convince the hearer how that applies to him.

A congregation will be very quick to detect if a preacher is preaching sermons that show evidence of his education or of his personal concern and conviction. Unless the preacher is convicted in his own heart, he will not be able to convince his hearer. Therefore, he needs to apply the message to his own heart before he applies it to others.

Whatever the cost, the preacher who applies the teaching of the Scripture to others must first be convicted by it and apply it to himself. Only he who has a personal knowledge and conviction of the sincerity and genuineness of the message he brings can persuade others of it.

This is the great need in our churches today, men who are convicted by the Holy Spirit of the truth that they preach, and then apply that truth to the congregation in such a way that they are also convicted. Jesus Christ applied the truth of His message to the circumstances and conditions of those to whom he spoke. The preacher must also do the same.

Assignment:

1. What is meant by the application?
2. Should every sermon have an application to both the believer and the unbeliever?
3. What are the conditions of a good application?
4. Listen to three sermons and examine how the application was made.

5.   Prepare a sermon outline on Matthew 22:34-40 and write out your application in full.

ILLUSTRATIONS

When our Lord Jesus Christ was preaching, He always used illustrations and parables, and great crowds came daily to listen to His words. The ability of the preacher to give an illustration to help his audience carry home the truth of the sermon will make his efforts more successful.

Although illustrations are a very effective way of helping to communicate the message to the hearer, a number of things must be taken into consideration about them.

1. The purpose of the illustration

As a house without a window to let in the light, is very dark, so also is a sermon without an illustration. Before using an illustration or story, we need to think carefully about the following:

a. **The illustration should make the point clear.** When Jesus was making clear the truths of the Gospel He used a parable, story or illustration. Therefore, an illustration should only be used when it will serve this purpose. Where the truth is plain there is no need of an illustration, but where it is useful it can be used.

When Jesus wanted to explain the union between Himself and the believer, He used the illustration, "I am the good Shepherd.

The good Shepherd lays down his life for the sheep" and "I am the door of the sheepfold." As soon as we hear these, we know immediately what they mean; they help us understand the truths they illustrate.

Jesus often used the word "like." He said, "the Kingdom of heaven is like..." We too need to add the word "like" in our sermons.

b. **The illustration may be used to prove the argument or statement.** Sometimes the sermon may be trying to point out a statement of fact from the Bible. The preacher may therefore be arguing his point but he may not get it clear to the audience, then an illustration may prove his point.

A preacher may be speaking on 1 Timothy 6:9, "Those who desire to be rich fall into temptation..." To prove his point he may use the story of Achan in Joshua 7:20-26. Again from 2 Kings 5:20-27 we read of the servant of Elisha, after Naaman was healed of leprosy.

c. **The illustration gives the congregation a rest.** A person cannot listen and concentrate continually for a long period of time. The mind needs a few moments to rest. If the preacher doesn't make that opportunity available in his sermon then the weary mind of the hearer will be forced to take it during the preaching.

Illustrations give the listener those few moments to relax from continuous concentration. He is then able to digest further deep studies of the Word of God.

d. **The illustration makes the message interesting.** It is difficult to make a congregation always interested in the sermon. Many people are not able or willing to listen to 30 minutes of an exposition of the Word of God.

Therefore, the preacher has to make it interesting by using an illustration to help aid the teaching contained in the sermon.

However, we should be careful that we do not preach a sermon consisting of many illustrations and stories with little or no exposition. This is more serious than having a sermon with no illustrations.

However, a well chosen and interesting illustration can suddenly make the uninterested or wandering mind pay attention to what is being said, and in doing so may be the means of changing his life for the good.

e. **The illustration can awaken and convince.** A preacher may faithfully preach the Word of God but fail to awaken or convince the hearer of his condition before God. The hearer may sit unmoved and think all this talk is for someone else.

However, the illustration may suddenly convey the truth to his heart. Is this not what Nathan did with David? When Nathan told David the story about the two men and the one ewe lamb, David's anger was greatly kindled against the man. He told Nathan, "As the Lord lives, the man who has done this deserves to die…" Then Nathan said to David, "You are the man…" The truth came immediately to David and he said, "I have sinned against the Lord."

A good illustration can sometimes do miracles in the lives of the hearers.

2. Illustrations should be short

Since the main purpose of the illustrations are to illustrate, clarify and help the congregation to understand the sermon then they should be short and not occupy a greater part of the address. The preacher must keep his illustrations brief and to the point. A sermon that is one long illustration or story after another is not an exposition of the Word of

God. The preacher will become known as a storyteller and not a man of the Word.

3. Illustrations should be accurate and honest

If the preacher is telling a true story then all the facts should be true, without exaggeration or addition. If he is giving facts then they should be true and complete. A preacher can do a lot of damage when he allegedly gives facts about a situation, and many members of the congregation know that these facts are not true or are distorted. This then puts doubt on the truth of the message he is trying to proclaim.

A preacher wants to impress them with the honesty, accuracy and integrity when giving illustrations and stories.

4. Care must be taken when using personal illustrations

Personal illustrations of the preacher can be helpful and give an understanding between the congregation and their pastor. If he can tell of something that he experienced or that had happened to himself or his family, it can make the illustration alive and real to everyone.

However, the preacher must **NEVER** speak about things he heard in confidence or rumours that someone told him. He must never speak about members of the congregation, their families or anything they had done. People will not share their lives and confidence with a pastor who may use this information in the pulpit.

5. Illustrations from the Bible

The student of the Bible will always have a good supply of illustrations. The Bible is full of stories, parables and illustrations to meet the need of any sermon, and these should be used to great advantage. Therefore, the preacher should always be thinking how he could illustrate what he is saying from the Scriptures.

6. General illustrations

The preacher can get illustrations from nature, magazines, newspapers and books. He should be interested in what he sees and reads. He can also make up his own illustrations. "Now let us suppose…" can lead into a most effective illustration to make clear a point in the sermon.

Assignment:

1.   What is the purpose of illustrations in a sermon?
2.   What are the qualifications of a good illustration?
3.   How should a preacher handle personal illustrations?
4.   From where did Jesus often take His illustrations?
5.   Listen to 3 sermons and see if the illustrations meet the conditions of a good illustration.

⌘

WRITING OUT OF THE SERMON

Preachers disagree on this matter of writing out the sermon. Some believe that all that is necessary is to have an outline. They do not approve of the writing out (or typing) the sermon in full because they claim that it restricts their freedom of thoughts and words when in the pulpit.

However, the advantages of writing out the sermon in full are greater than the disadvantages.

1. Writing makes the preacher think clearly

Any preacher who starts to write out his sermons in full will find it very difficult if not impossible at first. He will not be able to write everything that is needed to keep him preaching for 20 minutes. He will find it much easier just to preach his sermon. If, however, the sermon that is preached without being written out in full is compared to the one that is written, there is a great difference. The sermon that has been written out is much clearer and the content is expressed in greater detail because he has been forced to think out exactly what he wants to say.

2. The written sermon gives confidence to the preacher

The preacher who has written out his sermon in full will be able to preach much more confidently than one who has not done so. This is because he knows exactly what he is saying. It has all been prepared, it has been carefully written out and so there are no doubts or fears when it comes to preaching.

3. Be particularly careful in writing the introduction and conclusion

Great preachers have found it necessary to write out their sermons in full for some years at the beginning of their ministry, but as they developed and matured they would only write out one sermon each week and use detailed outlines for the other sermons.

However, the men who do this still prepare and write out in detail their introduction and conclusion. These are very important and cannot be left to the moment of preaching. We should always be careful about writing out the introduction and conclusion.

4. Writing develops the ability of the preacher

The more a preacher writes he develops his ability of expression. He learns to use words to express exactly what he means. He should be thinking, "does this word say exactly what I want to say?" "What other words would give the idea more clearly or express the fact more accurately?" We also need to ask, "Have I used the same words, or expression too many times?" "Where can I change the words to give variety?"

So often a preacher will repeat the same sentence or say the same thing many times in his sermon. He should be careful not to do this. This is why it is so useful to write out the sermon and read over it to see if we are repeating ourselves or expressing what we want to say in the best possible way.

The only way to improve our sermon preparation is to write and rewrite the sermons. Anyone who is seriously interested in preaching the very best sermons must spend much time in their preparation and writing out in full what he wants to say. There is no easy way to prepare sermons, and the preacher must be warned against the danger of falling into a careless habit of rushing through his preparation for one reason or another.

Assignment:

1.   What are the advantages in writing out the sermon?
2.   What would you consider are the disadvantages?
3.   How does someone improve his ability of writing sermons?
4.   How would you help someone who says he just cannot write out his sermon?

THE DELIVERY OF THE SERMON

Now that great care has been taken in the preparation of the sermon, it has to be preached to the congregation. A sermon that has a good outline and is well prepared will profit no one if it is badly preached. When a preacher delivers his sermon to a congregation, three different means of communication take place. The preacher should be careful how he uses them to the greatest benefit for the congregation. Let us now examine these in more detail.

1. The Preacher and his Words

The preacher has to use words to expound the Scriptures to the congregation. Therefore, he needs to be careful what words he uses. He must use words that everyone present can understand. Anyone who has been to school understands more words than someone who has never been to school. Also if someone has been to College or University he knows more than the person who has only been to primary school. What then about the preacher who has been to a Bible College? He will know many theological words and expressions that other people do not understand.

The preacher must deliver his message in simple words that the ordinary person uses in work, at the market or at home. A famous preacher who has more than one Doctorate degree said, "I have to study to be simple." What he meant was that with his education, he could very easily use big words that only educated people would know, but his purpose is to get the message to the ordinary person and so he must study and be careful to use simple language and words that his congregation understands.

There is no place in the pulpit for the preacher who wants to show to his congregation that he has been to college and now has a good education. Let him put his message into plain simple language.

However, the preacher must not be careless and use the same words over and over again. He can use a simple language in such a way that educated people can respect him for his ability. The formation of his sentences should be the very best. They should be clear and the grammar correct and he should preach in such a way that every word is heard clearly and understood. There is no place for a rambling preacher who uses badly planned and disconnected sentences.

Every preacher should think carefully about the words he is using to carry his message to the hearer. He is delivering a message from the Lord to people by means of a clear and simple language in words that everyone understands.

2. The Preacher and his Voice

If a preacher prepares his sermon well in simple language and no one is able to hear the message, it will profit nothing. The voice is the only means given to the preacher to deliver his message to the congregation. Therefore, he must use his voice in the best way to carry that message.

2.1. The voice should be heard clearly

It is very important that every member of the congregation hears the message clearly. There are three reasons why it could be difficult for a person to hear the preacher.

a. **The voice is too quiet:** When a preacher speaks quietly, there is the possibility that some people may not be able to hear him. The hearer may concentrate very hard to listen to the message but if he cannot hear the voice of the preacher then he has not profited from the message. The preacher should stand upright with his head up, and not always looking at his notes or the people in the front seats. He should look to the people in the back seats and speak clearly, as if he was speaking only to them.

b. **The voice is too loud:** It is difficult to hear clearly a preacher who shouts when he preaches. This is especially noticeable when it is a small Church building. The preacher should adjust the volume of his voice according to the size of the building or the number of people in attendance.

   Some people preach loudly because they think it gives them authority, but that is not so. Others shout when preaching to cover up for a loss of thought or nervousness.

   Every preacher must examine carefully the way he preaches so that the congregation can hear him clearly. If he speaks too quietly, they cannot hear and if he speaks too loudly, it is uncomfortable for the listener.

c. **He speaks too fast:** Some preachers begin to speak very fast when they get to the middle of their message. They are so much caught up in what they want to say that the words come tumbling out so fast that the congregation cannot hear him clearly. The preacher must be careful that he says each word clearly and distinctly. He must not speak too slowly as this is tiresome for the congregation, but he must not speak too fast that the words are not clear and plain for everyone to hear.

2.2. The pitch of his voice should be varied

To be an effective preacher the pitch of the voice will be used to help deliver the message. In normal conversation we raise and lower the tone of our voices. When we hear good news we give a shout in a high tone and if it is bad news we reply in a low tone. If we are not happy with someone then both the words and the tone with which we speak conveys the message very clearly.

Therefore, the preacher must raise and lower the tone of his voice when delivering his message. By speaking in a high tone or a low tone, in a voice that is not too loud or too soft he is able to convey the message much more effectively than just using words.

Care must be taken that he doesn't preach in what is known as a sing-song voice. Here the voice of the preacher rises and falls continuously as he preaches. He is not using his voice to emphasize what he is saying, but makes it go up and down at all times throughout the whole sermon. The preacher would not have an ordinary conversation with a friend in that tone of voice, so then he should not preach in this unnatural tone.

2.3. The speed should be varied

A preacher who goes on and on at the same speed and the same tone of voice, is very difficult to listen to. He needs to adjust his speed according to the message he is delivering. The variety of speed conveys different meanings and emotions.

When an illustration or story is being told it can be given at a good lively speed but when an important statement or conclusion given, it can be delivered at a lower speed. The sentences spoken more slowly stand out and emphasize importance to the hearer.

Sometimes a pause is very effective. The preacher, who speaks continuously without a pause, does not give the congregation a moment to think or digest what he has said. A pause before a statement calls attention to what the preacher is saying, and a pause after a story or statement adds importance to what has been said.

The preacher needs to be careful that the pause is just long enough to bring attention to what is being said and not so long that it is an embarrassing silence for the listener.

2.4. Do not let the voice drop

Some preachers drop their voice at the end of sentences. Others drop their voice deliberately during their preaching, thinking that it makes people concentrate on what they are saying. There are times when the voice should be lowered to help emphasize something but it should never drop to the point where people cannot hear what is being said. Everything the preacher says should be important, and if this is the case, then every word should be heard clearly and without difficulty or strain on the part of the hearer.

2.5. Do not repeat sentences

Some preachers repeat what they have said. They say it the first time in a normal tone and the next time say it louder and more forceful. Others will frequently say their statements twice or even three times in the same tone of voice. This is tiresome and annoying for the listener, who wants the preacher to get on with what he is saying and stop repeating himself.

Preachers can get into the habit of saying "In other words," "Let me explain it again," "Do you understand what I mean?" "Listen carefully to what I say" "Look! Do you see?" When these words are repeated throughout the sermon every week, they are a distraction for the regular Church member.

By repeating himself in this way, the preacher is able to make a ten minute sermon last for twenty minutes. It is not unusual to see a preacher look frequently at the clock in the Church and keep repeating what he has said until it is time for him to stop. A lazy preacher, because he has said everything in a few minutes needs to repeat himself to make his sermon last longer. Every preacher should examine himself and study how he preaches. If he writes out his sermon in full, he will not write the same thing several times. He will also have plenty to say and no need to repeat statements unnecessarily.

3. The Preacher and his Gestures

When a preacher is delivering his sermon, he must be active and use the movement of his body to help express and emphasize the message. Care must be taken that he doesn't move about so much and swing his arms around that it is a distraction to the message he preaches.

3.1. The preacher should stand at ease

The preacher should stand with his body upright and the feet slightly apart. This allows him to move his body freely and put action into his preaching. It has been known for preachers to stand with their legs crossed and elbow on the pulpit with head resting on the hand. This is a careless way to stand and gives the impression that what he is saying is not important.

A preacher with an urgent message to deliver cannot stand supporting his body against the pulpit in a lazy careless attitude. He needs to stand with his body free for action and show that he intends putting all his energy into what he is going to deliver.

3.2. A preacher should allow the arms freedom

If a preacher stands with his arms folded in front of him on the pulpit or with his hands in his pockets, he fails to impress the congregation of his seriousness. The use of the hands and arms can add meaning to the words that are spoken. When we explain to a stranger the road he is to travel we point with our finger the way he should go. If we are describing something that is long or wide, we extend out both arms out to add meaning to our description in words. When we want a child to come, we extend our hand out in invitation.

Just as these movements of the arms and hands add meaning to our conversation so they can be used very effectively in the pulpit. An active person maintains interest and holds attention to the listener. Therefore, a preacher should never preach behind a high pulpit. It should be low enough to give him freedom of movement and prevent him from resting on it. On the other hand, it should not be a low table as he has nowhere to place his Bible and notes to give him freedom of both hands.

Gestures can become a distraction if unnecessary and untimely actions become a habit. Some preachers swing their arms around every time they speak. As soon as they start to speak, the arm goes up and continues until the sentence is complete. To someone sitting listening and watching it becomes annoying, to the extent he has to turn his eyes from the preacher and only listen to his voice.

Gestures should be varied. The hand going up and down continuously brings attention to it and is unpleasant for the listener. However, well-timed expressions of one hand or the other or both hands together, with open hand, pointed finger and movement of the wrists can add meaning and purpose to the message.

3.3. The preacher should have eye contact with his congregation

Listeners who see the preacher "look at them in the eye" have greater personal contact with him than one who looks everywhere but at his audience. A person will listen with greater interest to the preacher who looks at him rather than over his head, or out of the window. Therefore, the preacher should move his eyes over the congregation let them rest on individuals here and there, to the left and to the right, to the front and to the back.

If the preacher is going to have eye contact with his congregation then he cannot have his eyes all the time on his sermon notes. As we have seen in lesson 14 it is good and necessary for the preacher to write out his sermon in full, but that does not mean he stands and reads it in the pulpit.

There are two ways of using the manuscript of a sermon after it is complete. The preacher can write the introduction in full, with the sermon outline or brief notes and the conclusion in full and carry this into the pulpit. He leaves his fully written out notes in his study. If he prepared his sermon well and read over his notes several times, then the brief notes or outline may be all he needs.

On the other hand, he may have more confidence if he carries the complete sermon into the pulpit. If he has read over it several times and is familiar with it then he can preach with only an occasional downward glance. This allows him to have eye contact with the audience.

3.4. The preacher should be serious

The preacher must convey to his congregation that he is serious in what he is saying. Where there is no zeal, no concern, no enthusiasm conveyed to the audience the sermon has lost much of its effectiveness.

On one occasion, an atheist went to hear a famous preacher and later someone said to him, "Surely you don't believe what that man was saying?" In reply he said, "No, but he did." Do we convey to our listeners that we believe what we are preaching?

We cannot preach on eternal matters without showing concern and seriousness on our faces. We cannot preach it with a smile. It is an urgent matter, and this is shown on our face when preaching. However, we cannot preach about the joys of eternal life and peace with God with a solemn and sad face. People don't want to watch and listen to a sad preacher. A preacher can be serious and at the same time show that he has got joy of the Lord in his heart.

Assignment:

1. Why must a preacher be careful about the words he uses?
2. How can a preacher deliver his sermon to be heard clearly?
3. How can a preacher use his voice to add emphasis to his message?
4. How should a preacher stand and use his arms when preaching?
5. Do you think it is necessary or important for the preacher to look at his congregation when speaking to them?

LESSON 16

PLAN A PREACHING PROGRAMME

Many preachers decide each week what they are going to preach on the Sunday. They choose the text or the topic for each sermon on a weekly basis. Some Churches have a preaching rota and each week has a different person to preach. That person is given the freedom to decide what he wants to speak on. However, the congregation who sits under the ministry of both these methods is not being cared for, and not being instructed in the Word of God as well as it could be if a preaching programme had been arranged. As the only spiritual food some Christians receive is what they get in Church on Sunday, it is a great responsibility on the preacher to plan what kind of food it is.

A preacher should discipline himself and study to take time to think and plan how he is going to teach and instruct the people under his care. Nothing can be planned successfully in a few minutes. It takes a lot of time but it is time well spent. He should pray over the matter, discuss it with elders and Church leaders; ask the members of the congregation to submit suggestions and requests; and then under the guidance of the Holy Spirit prepare a preaching plan. The plan may be detailed for three months, or six months with a general idea of his aim over the next one, two or three years.

When preparing a plan the following should be considered:

1. The preacher should have a general idea for one or two years ahead

We should say that in general the preacher should consider his ministry under four headings: devotional, evangelistic, ethical and doctrinal. Therefore, when planning a programme all four should be taken into consideration. If he is to preach the whole counsel of God then he cannot neglect any of them. At times it may not be possible to deal with them all in a three-month programme and so he should plan carefully, how he is going to cover them adequately over a period of one or two years.

This is a continuous process. We do not plan a programme once that covers a period of one or two years, and then when completed, just preach anywhere from the Bible week by week. The preacher should be thinking, planning, and have a general idea well in advance of what he proposes to do.

2. The preacher should consider exposition of the Scriptures

The preacher should prayerfully choose a book of the Bible and then expound it in sections or paragraphs to his congregation. On other occasions, he may select a number of chapters out of a book and expound them. Then after a period of about six months, he may want to return and continue. This prevents the congregation from getting tired of always dealing with the same book, and they welcome a change.

3. The preacher should take into consideration special days

The Christian year gives a good opportunity for the preacher to preach a series of sermons leading up to Easter, Christmas and other special days. Also he has Harvest Thanksgiving Day, Youth day, last Sunday of the year, New Year's Day and other occasions that the Church may arrange. These should be fitted into his preaching plan.

It has been known for a preacher to be preaching a series of sermons and when it came to the first Sunday of the New Year, he continued with his series without considering the occasion. Here he lost a good opportunity to his advantage.

4. The preacher should teach basic doctrine

Every year the preacher should teach, instruct and remind his congregation of the birth, death and resurrection, ascension and return of Christ. Also the doctrine of justification, repentance, sanctification, faith, grace, prayer and other important truths should be taught.

The preacher should see the need to bring constantly before his congregation the teaching of the Word of God. Unless they are reminded about these things, they may get careless and forget how important they are to their everyday living.

5. The preacher should teach ethical standards

As the preacher expounds the Word of God, he should teach ethics in both a personal and social situation. The Bible has much to say about Christian standards in the home and in society. Therefore, the preacher has a duty to teach and instruct his congregation on these matters.

6. The preacher should consider the Sundays and Wednesdays

When making a plan many things have to be taken into consideration. He has to think about the Sunday morning, Sunday evening and Wednesday services.

There are many ways of arranging the plan for Sunday morning and Sunday evening. While having an expository series in one he can have evangelistic messages in the other. While preaching on ethics in one he could have simple doctrine in the other. As Christians primarily attend the mid-week service the preacher has a unique opportunity to teach the "meat" of the Word, and Bible studies in greater depth.

The important thing is for the preacher to sit down and plan all his series to fit together to cover everything that needs to be preached or taught. If this is not done many important things will be neglected and the congregation will not be instructed in the whole Word of God.

7. The preacher should be careful about visiting speakers

Most congregations welcome visiting speakers to their pulpit and if this is included in the programme then it is good.

However, it is not good if there is a visiting speaker almost every Sunday and the preacher of the Church only preaches once or twice a month, divided among various meetings. After all, the preacher may have studied at a Bible College for up to three years and is trained for the job. However, if he has a rota of visiting speakers, who have no idea about preaching and very little knowledge about the Bible, then how will that help. This does not help in any way to the maturity and spiritual growth of the congregation?.

A preacher may get many requests from members or visitors, who want to preach in his Church, but he must be careful and not allow everybody and anybody to enter his pulpit. The elders should also be wise, and "jealously guard their pulpit" only allowing true men of God to enter and preach his Word. If a visiting speaker fails to reach the standard that is required, then no matter who he is, whether an elder, deacon or Church leader, he should be excluded from future plans.

Every faithful and dedicated preacher should think and plan, after much prayer, on the programme that he plans to use for all his Church meetings to the glory of God and edification of the saints.

Assignment:

1. Why should a preacher plan a preaching programme for his Church?
2. What should be considered when the plan is being made?
3. Suggest a plan you would make for your Church to last six weeks to deal with an important doctrine. What would be your subjects and Bible passages to be used?
4. Prepare a preaching plan for the exposition of 1 Peter: How many sermons would you have, and what would be your texts and themes?
5. Prepare a plan for your Church for Sunday morning, Sunday evening and Wednesday services to last 14 weeks from New Year's Day until Easter Sunday.

CONDUCTING CHRISTIAN WORSHIP

Jesus said. "It is written, 'you shall worship the Lord your God and Him only shall you serve'" (Luke 4:8). Again, Jesus said, "God is Spirit." If every Christian worshipped God and delighted to glorify and enjoy Him, then the preacher must think carefully what worship is, and how he can be a leader of worship.

1. What is worship?

Worship has often been spoken of as worth-ship or expressing worth to one who is worthy. In worship we recognize the merits of another. Worship is therefore the admiration or application to one who is worthy. When the wise men from the East came to Jesus, they fell down and worshipped Him. Then, opening their treasures, they offered Him gifts.

To worship means to do reverence, to adore, to pay homage. This is something that can mean more and have a higher value when we gather together as a company of God's people. We worship better as a congregation of Christians who are united in adoration of their creator and Lord. God is glorified in public worship. Just as a large crowd meets together to honour an important person, and the larger the crowd is the more important the person is, so when believers meet together in worship it shows how important their God is to them. The New Testament example shows that public worship is important and they did not have to be commanded to do it. It was something they did naturally, and it was a witness to outsiders.

The Psalmist says, "Offer to God a sacrifice of thanksgiving" (Psalm 50:14). In the book of Hebrews we are instructed to "continually offer a sacrifice of praise to God" (Hebrews 13:15). Thanksgiving and praise of God is part of worship. Worship is the offering of ourselves to God and ascribing to God the glory of His name.

The preacher or pastor is the leader of public worship and it is his responsibility to see that "all things should be done decently and in order" (1 Cor. 14:40). Again, he is instructed to see that, "When you come together, each one has a hymn, a lesson, a revelation, a tongue, or an interpretation. Let all things be done for building up" (1 Cor. 14:26).

The leader of public worship is to arrange or plan the parts of worship that should progress smoothly from beginning to the benediction. This is why the Apostle Paul instructed the Church at Corinth to see that "all things are done decently and in order." Many preachers think they only have to prepare their sermons, and give no thought or consideration to the various parts of worship.

It is common for a preacher to thoughtlessly announce the opening hymn, then ask someone to pray and then announce the second hymn and continue like this until the benediction. The hymns have been chosen by the choirmaster; the prayers spoken by an elder; the Bible reading by the preacher; the announcement by the Church Secretary and a special number requested by the congregation. Each person does his part with no consideration for how it joins what has happened before, or what will follow his part. God is pleased to see the things done in worship when they are done faithfully and from the heart. He loves sincere public prayer, Scripture reading, singing, the preaching of His Word and the giving of our gifts.

We will now consider the various parts that join to form a service of worship e.g. praise, prayer, the offering, reading of the Scripture and the sermon.

1.1. Praise in Worship

Praise is an important part of worship. Jesus and His disciples sang a hymn in the upper room (Mark 14:26). The believer is instructed to "sing Psalms and hymns and spiritual songs with thankfulness in your hearts to God" (Colossians 3:16).

Since the days of Moses, the people of God have the desire to praise the Lord. In Exodus 15, we have the song that Moses and the people of Israel sang to the Lord after they escaped from Egypt. So the Christian Church has inherited a long history of praise from Judaism. The New Testament pattern was congregational singing from the Psalms and hymns on Christian themes.

We are instructed to "continually offer up a sacrifice of praise to God, that is, the fruit of lips that acknowledge his name" (Hebrews 13:15). Praise therefore should be included in our worship of God. Praise helps us acknowledge the blessings of our Creator and Lord. If someone feels discouraged and sad and comes to a service of worship where the congregation enters whole-heartedly in praise to the Lord, then the person is blessed, uplifted and encouraged in the Lord.

Every service of worship should be a time when people are united in praise and thanksgiving to the Lord. If this is to be meaningful to everyone then a great responsibility rests on the preacher and the choirmaster.

a.   **Choose hymns or songs that are Scriptural.** When the book of Psalms is being used they address God in words inspired by His own Spirit. These then are very good to use in worship to praise God. However, if hymns and songs are used then the preacher has the responsibility to study the contexts to make sure they are scripturally sound. Some hymns cannot be usefully used in worship.

Hymns and songs need to be chosen that direct the mind to God. The message contained in them should be scripturally and doctrinally correct, and not lead people astray or teach error. Our praise should be directed towards God or the work of God and only hymns that do that should be chosen.

b. **Choose hymns or songs that are suitable.** Sometimes the preacher is seen looking through his hymnbook and selects the first hymn he knows and announces it to the congregation. The preacher and the choirmaster should discuss the theme for the sermon and what hymns or songs that could be sung to direct the minds of the worshipper towards the theme. Therefore, merely selecting any hymn is a wrong way to use the hymn book. Instead the chosen hymns or songs should have the theme of the message in mind and help in the smooth progress of the worship.

c. **Sing the hymns or songs lively.** It is surely wrong to sing hymns like, "Praise God from whom all blessings flow" or "Onward Christian soldiers" as if we were ready to fall asleep. These hymns should be sung at a good lively pace. They should be sung as if we mean what they say. We cannot look around us, or out of the window, or stand leaning against the wall and sing these great psalms or hymns in a meaningful way as part of our worship.

The preacher should teach the congregation how they can actively take part in a service of worship. The children of Israel joined together to sing praises to their Lord, so also should every member of the congregation today.

d.   **The responsibility of the choir.** In some Churches the congregation are expected to stand as the choir enters. There is no Scriptural justification for this action. This can lead to a wrong interpretation on the role of the choir. It can give the impression that they are important leaders in the Church and we stand to give them honour. There is no place for this attitude among an assembly of believers who are met to worship God.

The choir has the responsibility of leading the congregation in singing praises to God. They should choose a tune that can be easily sung and set the speed of the singing.

The choir may also be used to sing a special piece. Care must be taken that this is not a musical performance or entertainment but a part of the service of worship. The words should be sung clearly and the piece should be carefully chosen to help the congregation in their worship of God.

e.   **Having a special soloist or group singing.** In the service of worship, these can become a blessing or a hindrance. When the singers are introduced in the middle of a service of worship they can become the attraction or interest of the congregation, turning the congregation's mind and attention from God to man. This is a dishonour to the Name of Christ. When the congregation applaud the singers for their performance then it is a hindrance to the progress in the service of worship. When the pieces they sing are not firmly founded on the Scriptures, and sung for the praise and glory of God, then they should not be part of the service.

On the other hand, many people have been blessed and touched by the Spirit of God through the singing of a soloist or group. The preacher has the responsibility of doing what he feels, under the guidance of the Spirit, to be right.

1.2. Prayer in Worship

The New Testament Church was a praying Church. The Christians met together for prayer and also were taught to pray for individuals. When Jesus taught His disciples to pray He taught them to say "Our Father…" Christians should come together to pray and prayer is part of public worship.

Private prayer is the communication of the believer with his Lord. It is a personal matter when the believer cries out in private his praise, prayer, supplication and intercessions.

Public prayer in worship is different in that one person leads a congregation in prayer. Everyone joins in the same prayer. They are praying for the same thing at the same time. Jesus said, "If two of you agree on earth about anything they ask, it will be done for them by my Father in heaven" (Matthew 18:19). A preacher can lead his people to pray together about many different things. We must remember that public prayer is doing more than offering a private prayer in public. He is endeavouring to offer a prayer for all the people. Therefore, the leader of prayer is faced with this act of worship that is a great responsibility, and it cannot be done in a careless and unprepared way.

a.   **Public prayer should include all the main elements**

Paul wrote to Timothy saying, "I urge that supplications, prayers, intercessions and thanksgivings be made for all people…" (1 Timothy 2:1). It is important that prayer is not just a jumble of words and requests, but the basic elements, should be included.

i.   **Adoration.** To adore God is to worship and praise Him, to honour and exalt Him in our hearts and with our lips. The Bible teaches that God, our Father, desires the fellowship of His children. Our relationship to our heavenly Father should be one of complete trust, faith and obedience. We approach Him in adoration and praise, with reverence, love and gratitude. Our prayer should be an expression of our complete trust in Him and of the confidence that He hears us.

It is good therefore to commence a service of worship with adoration. This can be done either by the singing of a psalm or hymn by the whole congregation or by a prayer of adoration by the preacher. Here, he can list various attributes and works of the Lord for which He is to be praised.

A congregation that joins together with a psalm of adoration or a prayer led by the preacher at the beginning of the service of worship is drawn near to God and rejoices in His presence. It puts them into the right attitude of mind for the remainder of the service.

ii.   **Confession.** The psalmist said, "If I had cherished iniquity in my heart, the Lord would not have listened" (Psalm 66:18). Confessing sin prepares the heart for adoration, thanksgiving and supplication. But if we begin with adoration of God, any sin in our lives will be revealed by the Holy Spirit. For as we see God in His holiness and love, we become aware of our sin and unworthiness.

The preacher must take great care as he leads the congregation in the prayer of confession. They need to be taught not to confess sins in general but to be specific. At the same time confession of sin is a personal matter and every Christian should confess his own sins to the Lord. On occasions, it is profitable to have a few minutes silence when everyone present has an opportunity to seek the Lord personally.

iii.   **Thanksgiving.** We are commanded to "give thanks in all circumstances; for this is the will of God in Christ Jesus for you" (1 Thessalonians 5:18). To fail to give thanks is to disobey God. Grateful hearts will find no difficulty in listing spiritual and physical blessings and mercies for which to give thanks.

Giving thanks (also for our disappointment, trials and problems) demonstrates that we really trust God to do what is right and good. A father is always pleased when his children thank him for what he is doing for them. The Christian has cause to thank his heavenly Father. The preacher should lead his people in thanksgiving in the service of worship.

iv.   **Supplication.** We are commanded to pray for everything and in specific terms. Paul says, "do not be anxious about anything, but in everything by prayer and supplication with thanksgiving let your requests be made known to God" (Philippians 4:6). Supplication includes intercession for others and petitions for our own needs.

The Bible commands us to pray for:

a.   Those who mistreat us - *Matthew 5:44.*

b.   That we might not fall into temptation - *Matthew 26:41.*

c.   For the Lord's help for those who are sick or in trouble - *James 5:13.*

d.   For the rulers and those in authority over us - *1 Timothy 2:1-2.*

e.   For those who are serving God - *Romans 15:30-31, 2 Thessalonians 3:1.*

f.   That God, the Lord of harvest might send more workers - *Matthew 9:38.*

g.   For the millions in the world who do not know Christ.

h.   For the Church leaders.

b. **Public prayer should be orderly**

It is not possible for a congregation to enter into a prayer that goes from thanksgiving to confession and then jumps back to thanksgiving. All the sins to be acknowledged should be brought together in one prayer, and all the supplications and petitions in another.

Therefore, it is good to plan the various aspects of prayers in order. The first prayer may be adoration and praise; the second may be confession and thanksgiving, the third supplication and intercession, and a prayer of dedication after the offering. If an elder is being asked to pray then he should know and pray the type of prayer that fits into the service of worship.

c. **Public prayer should be definite**

Many public prayers are often too vague and general. The leader gives thanks "for all our blessings" or prays for God to "bless our nation" or "help the needy." These expressions fail to convict the congregation of the genuineness and reality of the prayer.

The leader of prayer must be specific enough to convince the congregation who is sharing in the prayer, of their own guilt, gratitude and concern for others that may be the content of the prayer.

All items that should be prayed for cannot be mentioned in every service of worship, but a few can be referred to, and others on another occasion. In the prayer of thanksgiving, a few items may be mentioned each Sunday. The same could apply to the prayer of adoration when divine attributes of God are mentioned. The leader of public prayer must therefore be specific and definite in his prayers.

Sometimes it is profitable for the congregation if the preacher announces the things for which he is going to pray. He could say,

Now in our prayer of intercession let us pray for those of
our congregation who are sick;

    for God's blessing upon our B.B company;

    for our special evangelism on Saturday afternoon;

    for the leaders of our nation;

    for the Christians in Government that they may be
faithful witnesses;

    for the spread of the gospel message in our land;

    for the Lord to help us so that we will not be ashamed
of Him. Let us now pray.

This now means that everyone is thinking about these items and
is sharing in the same prayer as the one who prays aloud.

d.   **Public prayer should be prepared**

If the preacher is to effectively lead his congregation in
prayer then he needs to prepare his prayers. If he fails to make
preparation they will gradually become a repetition week after
week of the same thing.

How then, can a preacher prepare his prayers for public
worship? First of all, it is clear that the more the preacher prays
in private the better he will pray in public. A preacher cannot
expect to pray well in public if he fails to practise prayer in his
private study. Again, a preacher who is close to the Lord and
studies his Bible will be a man who can pour out his heart to
the Lord in public. The prayers and petitions of various people
in the Scriptures give us an example to follow. If the preacher
is to include all the main elements in his prayers and if they are
to be orderly and definite, then he needs to decide in his study,
where and how he is going to do this. As we have seen in lesson 14
that writing out the sermon in full helps the preacher to express
himself, so it could also be applied here. While in the study if

the preacher writes out a prayer and examines it then it will help him to express himself better and avoid repetition. The important thing is that he knows exactly what he is going to include in each prayer in his order of service.

e. **Public prayer should be heard**

In many Churches it is the practice to ask an elder or other member to pray, but the contribution of that prayer to the worship is very small, because no one can hear what he says and it amounts to four or five minutes of silence in the Church with a mumble from the place where someone is praying.

When a person is asked to pray in public he should stand up, face the congregation and speak loudly and clearly for everyone to hear. He should also know the type of prayer in which he is being asked to lead.

f. **Public prayer should not be too long**

Sometimes the person who prays goes on and on especially in the prayer of intercession. He tends to go around the whole world before he stops. This causes the congregation to get tired and they can no longer participate in the prayer.

It is much better to have short prayers where everyone can take an active part, than long prayers where people can allow their thoughts to wander to other things. (In the weekly Church meeting, it is also more lively and challenging when many people take part in short prayers for a specific item than a few people praying long prayers that cover many items).

g. **Part of public prayer may be silent**

As the leader of public prayer cannot know the burdens in the heart of the congregation, it may be useful and profitable if an opportunity is given for the individual to make his own prayer request before the Lord.

The leader may suggest we all pray in the silence of our own hearts. Giving thanks for God's blessings upon us and our family and laying before Him any burden or request that we so desire. Then a brief moment (about two or three minutes) of silence is given for everyone to pray personally to the Lord. This may prove to be a very valuable time for the congregation when they can actually take an active part in the prayers, even though it may be in the silence of their own hearts.

1.3. The Offering in Worship

Some people do not include the offering in their service of worship, but the offering should be seen, not as a "collection" but an act of worship, like praise and prayer.

Christian giving is a privilege and responsibility. Everything that is on earth belongs to God, He created everything. But for the Christian he has experienced a new birth, he has become an heir with Christ in glory. It is through the sacrifice and death of Christ that the Christian has been given his new life. It then follows that we should be willing, and with a cheerful heart, give back to God part of what He has given to us.

When we were born into this world, we were naked physically and we owned no money or possessions. During the years since birth, we have acquired money and possessions through gifts, inheritance and work. We must not forget then that God has given all we have to us. We have been entrusted with money and possessions and if Jesus is Lord of our life then some of these should be given back to Him.

In Proverbs 3:9 we are instructed to "Honor the Lord with your wealth and with the first fruits of all your produce" and as a reward we are told, "then your barns will be filled with plenty and your vats will be bursting with wine."

Again in Malachi 3:10 we are instructed to "Bring the full tithe into the storehouse, that there may be food in my house." Then we are told, "Thereby put me to the test, says the Lord of hosts, if I will not open the windows of heaven for you and pour down for you a blessing until there is no more need."

a.   **The purpose of the offering**

Throughout the Bible, giving and offerings are part of worship. In the Old Testament, the Levites were set apart for the service of the sanctuary. They were to be maintained by the offerings the people brought to the house of God. This did not change in the New Testament Church. When Paul wrote to the Christians at Philippi he said, "I have received full payment, and more; I am filled, having received from Epaphroditus the gifts you sent, a fragrant offering, a sacrifice acceptable and pleasing to God" (Philippians 4:18). Therefore, supporting, the preacher and the expenses of the Church, missionary work and the spread of the gospel; helping the poor and the needy, widows and the fatherless is not just helping from a generous heart, but is to take part in an offering to the Lord and an act of worship.

b.   **The way to give offerings**

There is a wrong way and right way of doing everything and this also applies to the offering.

i.   **The wrong way.** Some people give as little as possible. They consider all the money and possessions they have to be their own. They only give a very small amount to the Lord's work. But those who give little do not realize they will only get little in return, but he who gives freely to God will gain even more.

However, other people want to give so that it will be seen or known how much they gave. But Jesus said, "Be careful not to do your 'acts of righteousness' before men to be seen by them. If you do, you will have no reward from your Father in heaven…" (Matthew 6:1-4).

ii.   **The right way.** It is only when we give in the right way we receive a blessing and a reward. When Paul was writing to the Corinthians he explained how the Christians from the Macedonian Churches had given, and how their way should be an example to the Christians at Corinth.

In Corinthians chapters 8 and 9 we read how the Christians gave joyfully, sacrificially, of their own freewill, whole-heartedly, and they gave themselves to the Lord. The Christian is taught to decide for himself how much he should give and he should give in secret.

Many preachers criticize the people at the offering about their poor giving and then plead with them and demand that they give more. But if the members of the congregation are to give according to the teaching of the Scriptures then they should have teaching on stewardship and tithing. The time before the offering is not the time to complain about their poor giving. This will not help them to give cheerfully or willingly.

The offering should be seen to be part of the service of worship. Therefore, the preacher should not say "Now is the time for the collection…" but he may say, "Let us worship God with our offerings…" and the Christian will count it a privilege and joy to give unto the Lord.

1.4. The Reading of the Scriptures in Worship

The Scriptures were read in the Synagogues while the congregation listened. Now today we also include the public reading of the Scriptures in worship. The Scriptures are the divinely inspired revelation of God and the Christian believes God's voice can speak through that written record.

Although it is probably true that almost every home has a copy of the Bible, this does not mean everyone reads the Bible. The Bible would not be read frequently by the unconverted and the illiterate cannot read it, therefore the only time they may hear it read is in the Church.

a. **Public reading of the Scriptures should be the result of careful preparation**

Before the preacher reads the Scriptures in public, he should make careful preparation. He should be aware of the fact that this is the Word of God. Therefore he should read it privately until the message grips his own heart, then he can read it publicly in a way that it will grip the heart of the hearer.

It is sad to hear preachers stumbling and stammering through a portion of the Scripture. How can such a thing be profitable to the hearer? The preacher should read the passage of Scripture several times aloud in his study or from the pulpit of the Church, when no one is present. To read it silently is not good preparation. It is only when he reads it aloud that he can know how to use his voice to express a good reading of the passage.

The reading of the Scriptures should be loud and clear for everyone to hear. To pronounce words wrongly can be disastrous and give the wrong meaning from the passage. The words should be pronounced clearly and definitely. If this is done then the public reading of the Scriptures will be a delight to the congregation and a part of worship.

b. **Care must be taken about the length of the passage**

Preachers have been guilty of two extremes in respect of the length of passage they read. Some have been known to read one or two chapters while others will read only one or two verses. It is obvious that two chapters are too long and two verses too short.

The passage should be long enough to give those who only hear the Scriptures read in Church something to think about and remember. It is doubtful if this could be less than ten verses. On the other hand, if it is too long the congregation may lose interest and become restless. Much depends on how the passage is read. If the reading is not good then their patience will not bear with the reader, but if it is well read then they may want to listen to a longer passage.

Reading the Scriptures is a very important part of public worship. The preacher must think carefully and prayerfully how he can do it to the glory of God.

1.5. The Place of the Sermon in Worship

Some people do not see the sermon as part of the service of worship. They see it as an opportunity for the preacher to express his mind and feeling to the congregation. If a service is to be shortened because of time, it is usually the sermon that is reduced to a few comments.

In these notes we have studied in great detail the preparation of the sermon, because it is so important, not as a special part of a service but as a part of the complete service of worship.

The sermon is an act of worship when it is developed from the Scriptures and the preacher is speaking as a representative of God. He is not giving his own message, but is the messenger delivering what he has received from God. As a result the minds of the hearers are turned to God. Where the sermon does this, it is an act of worship.

Again, the sermon must be the result of much prayer. A sermon that is made in the wisdom of man will fail to be an act of worship. A sermon prepared without prayer becomes a speech or talk to an audience but a message that comes through meditation and prayer is used by God to speak to the hearts of the hearer, and they respond in worship.

A sermon may be well prepared through prayer, and well delivered but fail to affect the congregation if the Holy Spirit does not take the message and speak to the heart of the hearer. It is the Holy Spirit who makes the sermon fruitful. Therefore, every preacher should see that he needs the presence of the Holy Spirit with him when delivering the sermon. He needs to pray as he enters the pulpit that the Holy Spirit will take him and use him for the glory of God.

When the members of the congregation feel themselves in the presence of God and want to respond to Him then the sermon becomes an act of worship. The preacher has a great responsibility of bringing the worshipper to worship God, and the sermon is one of the means at his disposal. "Faith comes from what is heard, and what is heard comes by the preaching of Christ" (Romans 10:17).

A service of worship has various parts that are not separate items but join together to form a unit: praise, the offering, reading of the Scriptures and the sermon all join together to form a service of worship. May every preacher study and work on all aspects of worship and see himself not as the preacher of a sermon, but the leader of worship.

Assignment:

1. How can a preacher prepare for a service of worship?
2. Explain the part praise has in worship.
3. How should public prayers be conducted?
4. How would you explain to your congregation that the offering is part of worship?
5. What preparation should be done before the Scriptures are read in public?
6. How does the sermon fit into a service of worship?

CONCLUSION

God has chosen the "foolishness of preaching" as the means whereby the gospel message is known to mankind. "How are they to hear without a preacher?" is the question that is asked by the Apostle Paul. This is a great responsibility laid upon the preacher.

It is true to say there are men occupying the pulpits of our Churches today who have never been converted and have never been called to be a preacher. They have not had a personal encounter with Christ, how then can they persuade others to seek the Saviour? Paul was very concerned about this when he said, "I discipline my body and keep it under control, lest after preaching to others I myself should be disqualified" (1 Corinthians 9:27).

On the other hand there are men in teaching, trading and in business whom God has called to be preachers but they have rejected it. Some complain the money is not good, that the Church cannot pay a good salary. Others have various reasons and excuses for not taking up the work of a preacher. Samuel told Saul, "Behold to obey is better than sacrifice." The Lord is looking for those who are obedient and willing to do His will in their lives. Men and women are crying out because of their lost condition but there is no one to lead and instruct them. May God send forth more labourers in His field.

After studying these notes, you will have seen that taking up the work of a preacher is no small thing. It requires a great deal of hard work. Perhaps you have been a preacher for many years but your zeal is not as great today as it has been in the past. We pray that these studies will help to renew that zeal and give you the needed encouragement to do it.

If you are an experienced preacher then it is good to have regular evaluation of your preaching. You may develop habits and methods and be unaware of it. You may not agree with everything that is in these notes but they could be the instrument God uses to make you think and consider how efficiently you are doing your work. These notes will make you think things out clearly for yourself. They do not say everything that could be said about homiletics. As the title states they are "Preliminary" notes. They are for the beginner and are written in a simple clear way for everyone to understand.

We pray that your ministry will be enriched by what you have studied and you have been encouraged to see the great task you are involved in can be done by the help of the Holy Spirit.

May we hear the words of our Master: "Well done good and faithful servant."

BIBLIOGRAPHY

Adam, Peter. *Speaking God's Words: A Practical Theology of Expository Preaching.* Regent College Press, 2004.

Adams, Jay E. *Preaching With Purpose.* Zondervan, 1986.

Akin, Daniel L. *Engaging Exposition.* B&H Academic, 2011.

Alexander, James W. *Thoughts on Preaching.* Banner of Truth Trust, 1984.

Ash, Christopher. *The Priority of Preaching.* Christian Focus, 2009.

Balchin, J.F. *Understanding Scripture.* Inter-Varsity Press, 1981.

Barker, Paul A., Condie, Richard J., and Malone, Andrew S. (ed.). *Serving God's Words: Windows on Preaching and Ministry.* Inter-Varsity Press, 2011.

Berghoef, Gerald and Dekoster, Lester. *The Elders Handbook.* Christian's Library Press, 1979.

Blackwood, A.W. *The Fine Art of Preaching.* Baker Book House, 1976.

Braga, J. *How to Prepare Bible Messages.* Multnomah Press, 1969.

Broadus, J.A. *On The Preparation and Delivery of Sermon.* Harper and Row Publisher, 1979.

Capill, Murray. *The Heart is the Target.* P & R Publishing, 2014.

Carrick, John. *The Imperative of Preaching.* Banner of Truth, 2003.

Carson, H.M. *Hallelujah – Christian Worship.* Evangelical Press, 1980.

Chapell, Bryan. *Christ-Centred Preaching.* Baker, 2005.

Clowney, Edmund P. *Preaching Christ in All of Scripture.* Crossway, 2003.

Coffin, H.S. *The Public Worship of God.* Independent Press Ltd, London, 1950.

Coggan, Donald. *Stewards of Grace.* Hodder & Stoughton, 1958.

Davis, Dale Ralph. *The Word Became Fresh.* Mentor, 2006.

Day, David. *A Preaching Workbook*. SPCK Publishing, 2004.

Dever, M. and Gilbert, G. *Preach: Theology Meets Practice*. B&H, 2012.

Dumas, Dan. *A Guide to Expository Ministry*. SBTS Press, 2012.

Evans, W. *How to Prepare Sermons*. Moody Press, 1964.

Gibbs, Alfred P. *The Preacher and His Preaching*. Walterick Publishers, 1939.

Gibbs, Alfred P. *Worship*. Walterick Publishers, 1960.

Goldsworthy, Graeme. *Preaching: The Whole Bible as Christian Scripture*. Eerdmans, 2000.

Green, Christopher and Jackman, David (ed.). *When God's Voice is Heard: The Power of Preaching*. Inter-Varsity Press, 2003.

Gunn, J. *If Any man Speak*. Everyday Publications Inc., 1969.

Handerson, G. *Lectures To Young Preachers*. B. McCall Barbour, 1961.

Helm, David R. *Expositional Preaching*. Crossway, 2014.

Henrichsen, W.A. *A Layman's Guide to Interpreting the Bible*. Zondervan/ Navpress, 1976.

Johnson, Darrell W. *The Glory of Preaching: Participating in God's Transformation of the World*. IVP Academic, 2009.

Keller, Timothy. *Preaching: Communicating Faith in an Age of Scepticism*. Hodder & Stoughton, 2015.

Kendall, R.T. *Tithing*. Hodder and Stoughton, 1982.

Lane, Denis. *Preach The Word*. Evangelical Press, 1979.

Lawson, Steven J. *The Kind of Preaching God Blesses*. Harvest House, 2013.

Lloyd-Jones, D. Martyn. *Preaching & Preachers*. Zondervan, 1972.

Logan Jr., Samuel T. (ed.). *The Preacher and Preaching*. P&R Press, 1986.

MacArthur, John. *Preaching: How to Preach Biblically*. Thomas Nelson, 2005.

MacArthur, John. *Rediscovering Expository Preaching*. Thomas Nelson, 1992.

Mawhinney, Bruce. *Preaching With Freshness*. Kregel, 2008.

Meyer, Jason C. *Preaching: A Biblical Theology*. Crossway, 2013.

Millar, G. and Campbell, P. *Saving Eutychus*. Matthias Media, 2013.

Mohler Jr., R. Albert. *Feed My Sheep: A Passionate Plea for Preaching*. Reformation Trust Pub., 2008.

Motyer, J. Alec. *Preaching?: Simple Teaching on Simply Preaching*. Christian Focus, 2013.

Msweli, S. and Crider, D. *The Shepherd and His Work*. Evangel Publishing House, 1974.

Olford, Stephen F. and Olford, David L. *Anointed Expository Preaching*. B&H, 2003.

Olford, Stephen F. *The Grace of Giving*. Lakeland, 1972.

Olyott, Stuart. *Preaching Pure and Simple*. Bryntirion Press, 2005.

Piper, John. *The Supremacy of God in Preaching*. Baker, 2004.

Richard, Ramesh. *Preparing Expository Sermons*. Baker, 2001.

Robinson, Haddon W. *Biblical Preaching*. Baker, 2001.

Rummage, Stephen N. *Planning Your Preaching*. Kregel, 2002.

Sangster, W.E. *The Craft of Sermon Construction*. Pickering & Inglis, 1978.

Sangster, W.E. *The Craft of Sermon Illustration*. Pickering & Inglis, 1978.

Scharf, Greg. *Prepared to Preach*. Christian Focus, 2005.

Shaddix, James L. *The Passion-Driven Sermon*. Broadman and Holman, 2003.

Spurgeon, C. H. *Lectures to My Students*. Zondervan, 1979.

Sterrett, T. Norton. *How to Understand Your Bible*. Inter-Varsity Press, 1974.

Stewart, James S. *Heralds of God*. Regent College Publishing, 1946.

Storrs, Richard S. *Preaching Without Notes*. University of Michigan, 2006.

Stott, John R. W. *Between Two Worlds*. Eerdmans, 1982.

Sunukjian, Donald. *Invitation to Biblical Preaching*. Kregel, 2007.

Torrey, R.A. *How to Work for Christ*. Nisbet & Co. Ltd, 1901.

Tozer, A.W. *Gems from Tozer*. Christian Publications, Inc., 1969.

Webley, S. *How to Give Away your Money*. Inter-Varsity Press, 1978.

White, R.E.O. *A Guide To Pastoral Care*. Pickering & Inglis Ltd., 1976.

White, R.E.O. *A Guide To Preaching*. Pickering & Inglis Ltd., 1973.